Pure
CALIFORNIA

Pure CALIFORNIA

35 Inspiring Houses In The New California Tradition

BASSENIAN / LAGONI ARCHITECTS

A Book By Bassenian/Lagoni Architects
Copyright © 2003 by Bassenian/Lagoni Architects (hardcover)
Copyright © 2004 by Bassenian/Lagoni Architects (softcover)

Library of Congress Control Number:
2002110994

International Standard Book Number:
0-9721539-0-X (hardcover)
0-9721539-1-8 (softcover)

Published by Bassenian/Lagoni Architects
2031 Orchard Drive, Suite 100
Newport Beach, CA 92660-0753
Phone: 949-553-9100
Fax: 949-553-0548
bassenianlagoni.com

Corporate
Chairman & CEO: Aram Bassenian, AIA
President: Carl Lagoni, AIA
Executive Vice President: Lee Rogaliner
Senior Principals: Scott Adams, AICP
               David Kosco, AIA
               Jeffrey LaFetra, AIA

Book Production
Editorial Director: Aram Bassenian, AIA
Editor-in-Chief: Rickard Bailey, Bailey Consulting, Inc.
Writer: Laura Hurst Brown, Brownhurst Enterprises
Design/Art Director: Edie Motoyama
Art Director/Designer, Cover Design: Zareh Marzbetuny, ZM Design
Plan Graphics: Jennifer Cram
Editorial Coordinator: Debby Owens
Assistant to the Editorial Director: Kele Dooley
Print Consultant: Dedra Smith, Printmark

Color Separations by Toppan Hong Kong

Printed in Hong Kong by Toppan Printing

10 9 8 7 6 5 4 3 2

Contents

Chapter Three

California Coastal Homes

Chapter Four

Small-Lot Detached Homes

Foreword

A New Breed of Residential Architect
by Howard Englander

As the poet scratches words across the empty page to pen a moving verse and as the artist lays oils upon the empty canvas to illuminate emotion and the moment, so too does the architect carve lines and sculpt forms to shape a house. The "house," more than a shelter from cold and haven from the wind and rain, symbolizes a dream, a sacred place whose character, style and contours evolve from the architect's ingenuity and visionary power.

To birth a house—to forge and organize an unruly array of lines and dimensions that compose and define "home"—constitutes artistry, a work dependent upon the creative daring of one individual. Names like Wright, Neff and Greene all resound as creators who aligned shape and form to elevate architecture to art. Their expression was multidimensional, often unconstrained by conventional and traditional thinking, always seeking to venture into unexplored terrain. Architecture is the ultimate and quintessential "public art piece." It textures and backdrops everyday life, every hour, every moment.

Today a new breed of residential architect has emerged. Their task demands the same intensity or creative vision that distinguishes the work of the architectural legends who designed one home at a time on one single piece of property. However, this new generation has been charged with a much more significant task. Their energies have been directed at conceptualizing and designing communities whose final aesthetic is a composite of elements where architecture and planning organically amalgamate to frame a sense of place—a living environment.

One architectural firm that exemplifies the artistic mastery of traditional architecture while adventuring into a whole new dynamic arena of residential design is Bassenian/Lagoni Architects. This powerful architectural firm, founded by Aram Bassenian, is guided by the inspired leadership of Aram and Carl Lagoni and furthered by a talented cadre of principals, associates, architects and planners. This imaginative team has pioneered a multitude of unique and bold ideas that have immeasurably influenced and impacted residential architecture in California, throughout the United States and now overseas. The delicate mix of artistic whimsy and a reverence for historic architectural influences differentiates and elevates their rich body of work. Testimony to Bassenian/Lagoni Architects' many achievements are the beautiful homes and thriving communities which the firm has designed throughout California, the country and around the world.

Bassenian/Lagoni Architects' bold and cutting-edge achievements have set a heightened standard which the housing industry has honored by a deserved multitude of awards and accolades. Several of their residential projects act as architectural paradigms, symbolizing design excellence and conceptual breakthroughs, and generating an unrivaled collection of trend-setting residential projects. These endeavors span across the full design spectrum and include single-family homes whose brilliance surpasses many custom residences to higher-density, attached housing which sensitively joins home and "place" to ensure an enriching neighborhood environment.

Bassenian/Lagoni Architects are leaders and committed advocates of the principle that architecture and planning represent a fully integrated discipline. Their purpose and ideal is to intensify the quality of neighborhood fabric as expressed by a powerful aesthetic, merging land form and architectural form to create enduring communities. These remarkable achievements are Bassenian/Lagoni Architects' own enduring legacy.

Introduction
by Aram Bassenian, AIA

Our work began in the early seventies. Energized by the social consciousness and idealism of the previous decade and a commitment to actively participate in solving the nation's housing needs, we found our opportunity in production housing. Here was an industry that had very little involvement by trained design professionals, but a major impact on our national built environment. And California, with its dynamic economy, growing populations, and desirable casual lifestyle, was poised to become the national incubator for new ideas in residential architecture.

At a time when most of our colleagues were concentrating on one-of-a-kind solutions, we saw the potential that came with mass production and unabashedly joined the ranks of those who embraced that direction. The appeal was the ability to effect positive change for a large segment of our population by extending the architect's professional skills and improving the American at-home experience.

From the beginning, we recognized that the catalysts for improvement were California's temperate climate and its free spirit. We surrounded ourselves with the most talented people we could find—architects who shared our passion for housing—then created a professional yet caring atmosphere and encouraged a culture rooted in innovation. We upheld the virtues of clear logic, efficiency, furnishability, and a balanced allocation of space.

Our overriding philosophy was that livability should be the primary motivator for our residential design. We began to focus on family lifestyle and concentrated heavily on the development of the informal zone. We paid homage to those pioneering architects who had preceded us by further opening the plan. We determined not to be satisfied with merely solving the problem—but encouraged whimsy and delight as an integral part of an exciting architecture. And we advocated a process where design begins on the inside and the exterior forms are then allowed to follow. We understood early on that we had to remain market-sensitive yet innovative in design—all the while promoting simplicity and discipline in construction methods and, as a result, helping to control budgets.

And all along, it was our desire to take production housing away from its shelter-only beginning. With individuality, character, exciting spatial composition, and with elevations that deliver a strong emotional impact, we attempted to melt away the negative, stereotypical stigma associated with the formative work that occurred in our industry.

During the economically volatile early eighties, in order to achieve affordability, we offered the industry hope in the form of pragmatic yet exciting alternatives on smaller lots. Our designs offered value—they lived and felt bigger than they were. We gained national recognition for our inventiveness and leadership in developing homes that functioned well within constrained dimensions. Later in the same decade, during an expanding economy, our emphasis naturally shifted to larger and more sophisticated homes. We learned to be team players with the best builders and market analysts in the country and we gained a wealth of knowledge from those great associations. We also benefited tremendously from our collaborations with top professionals in related fields—structural engineers, interior designers, and landscape architects. As a result, we were recognized as the best of our class—and nationally reputed to be among the design leaders of the luxury production market.

During the more difficult housing environment of the early nineties, our firm advanced the idea of built-in flexibility. Our homes evolved to lose some of their rigidity and the pieces became less defined by specific use and thus more adaptable to each homeowner's changing needs.

Along the way, treading lightly through continent-sized shifts in

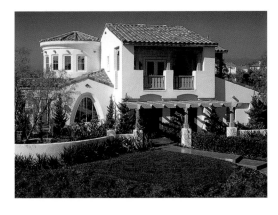

demographics, we persistently sought creative solutions for urban and mid-urban infill locations. Here, whether with higher density detached homes or multi-family answers, it was our aim to respond with contextual solutions that gently blended into the fiber of existing communities. With a zeal for creative land planning and a desire for timeless architecture rendered in refined details and classic proportions, we strove to achieve designs that would have a positive impact on existing neighborhoods.

In the mid-nineties, with a substantial presence in the American Sunbelt, we were self-confident enough to be introspective and, along with other colleagues in our profession, paused to question our work, discovering a few flaws in our craft. We found ourselves embedded in a quagmire of formula floor plans and stale elevations.

We realized that it was not enough to simply modify our *house designs*, our mandate now was to change and improve the *overall community*. Our vision had to be expanded beyond the confines of the individual home. Each residence had to be designed to respect and enhance the collective streetscape and the dominance of the three-car garage had to be minimized. Variation in the massing of each home and diversity in exterior styling along with four-sided architecture had to be achieved in order to bring back our beautiful streets. It was time to go back to our roots and honor the age-old idea that good design should evidence a correct response to the climate and display a reverence for regional and historic context.

Within our firm, a call-to-arms went out to battle sameness. It was a cry for creativity, to cultivate diversity. It was time for a change. And the awakening that followed was a rebirth that gave life to an ocean of new ideas.

With an eye toward changes in demographics and keenly aware of the necessity for privacy between increasingly diminished lots,

we began to explore and analyze the time-honored designs of houses and communities in Europe, particularly Spain, Italy and France. We also revisited our own beginnings by carefully studying early California, Santa Barbara and Mission vernacular styles. Empowered by this research, we began to discover a multitude of new ways to introduce natural light to the core of our floor plans. By modifying the perimeter and re-introducing the age-old concept of the courtyard, playful light combined with modulation in interior volume came back to break the grapples of convention. The resultant designs, replete with extended sight lines and sequential series of surprising architectural experiences, have re-organized our floor plans and energized the residential landscape. These changes have struck a resonant chord, not only with California homeowners, but also with buyers in a number of communities throughout the United States and even abroad.

In the pages that follow, accompanied by complimentary observations from our writer, Laura Hurst Brown, we are pleased to present a selection of homes that represents the most interesting of our recent body of work. Although our practice includes a wide variety of sizes and types within the residential spectrum, for these pages we have chosen, with only a few exceptions, a concentration of detached homes designed in the production format. And while the exterior elevations featured here reflect only three families of style, it is important to mention that our palette stretches wider than the sampling shown in this volume. Our years of experience in housing have ingrained in us an attitude of openness toward design and a philosophy that welcomes inevitable change.

Chapter One

EARLY CALIFORNIA HOMES

A house expresses history in its most intimate form. California's architecture connects a diverse genealogy and geography, and speaks volumes about its singular beginnings. Deeply rooted in centuries-old Hispanic vernaculars, a rich weave of bucolic patios, masonry arches, and barrel-tile roofs shape the venerable structures that are today's state treasures. In the early 20th Century, a compendium of East Coast and European styles collided with the sleek, simple lines of ranch houses and haciendas, creating a new breed of design. Colonial houses shed their staid proportions to take in the scale of the wide-open spaces and a vocabulary of revival dialects was born. Reinvented Mission and Monterey designs by Golden Age architects such as Wallace Neff and Lilian Rice begat a sea change in elite communities like Rancho Santa Fe, Pasadena and Santa Barbara—cities that today resolve high-density conditions with fresh interpretations of courtyard styles. The collection of historic designs on the following pages breaks new ground with uncommon blends of Moorish and Andalusian influences, cantilevers and pavilions, courtyards and porticos, cozy sheltered spaces and untamed views.

Windward at Crystal Cove RESIDENCE ONE

LOCATION: NEWPORT COAST, CALIFORNIA
BUILDER: RICHMOND AMERICAN

PHOTOGRAPHY: ERIC FIGGE 2001

3,466 SQUARE FEET

With the elegance of a rustic villa, this revival home mixes high-tech luxury with historic ingenuity. A single-story plan in this coastal community, the home employs 10-foot ceilings to enhance its sense of spaciousness and increase views and outdoor flow.

Windward at Crystal Cove Like an ancient bell wall, the forward gable of this Spanish Colonial façade guards a cache of serene garden and interior spaces. Integrating a variety of Early California elements, the elevation is unified by the use of arches, plain wall surfaces and clay-tile roofs. Rich with revival instincts, this reinvented Mission design embraces a quiet palette of cool stucco and native wood. Powerful forms, both familiar and new, meld with the serenity of a central courtyard that opens from each of the living spaces.

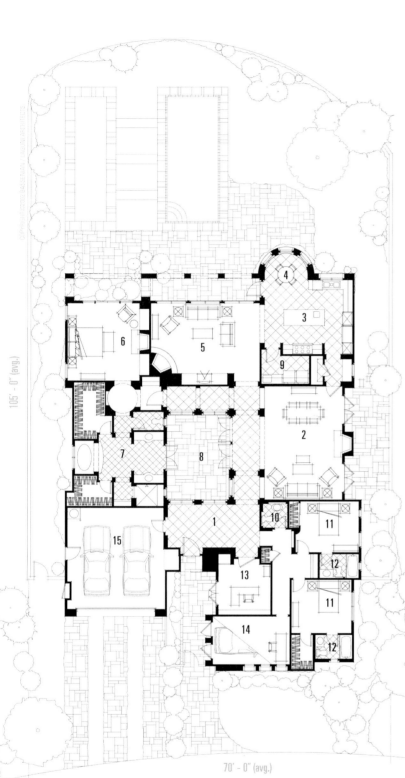

105' - 0" (avg.)

70' - 0" (avg.)

Influenced by the historic architecture of Santa Barbara, this 21ˢᵗ-century home introduces a gentle mix of Old World and California country elements.

1	Entry	9	Laundry
2	Living/Dining Room	10	Powder Room
3	Kitchen	11	Bedroom
4	Nook	12	Bathroom
5	Family Room	13	Office
6	Master Suite	14	Garage/Studio
7	Master Bathroom	15	Garage
8	Courtyard		

Asymmetrical shed and gable roofs, ironwork grilles and the modern vertical proportions of the elevation are rooted in Andalusian design. Mosaic tile surrounds the entry, suggesting a Moorish influence. Tall windows and slender arches intimate the colonnades of New World missions, while flush rakes and exposed rafter tails articulate an Early California vocabulary. Nested in the coastal hills between Newport Beach and Laguna Beach, the site is oriented to the southwest—facing the Pacific—to maximize views and sunlight. Location and lifestyle provide the context for placing the informal spaces to the rear of the plan, which overlooks the entertainment terrace, pool and spa. A loggia protects the southwestern elevation from

Daylight is softly filtered into the interior spaces through the open center courtyard—a serene outdoor living room that eases the transition between private and public realms. French doors can remain open even on cloudy days to bring in natural light and improve circulation throughout the interior.

A sleek functional space, the gourmet kitchen overlooks a morning bay and views of the Pacific. Subdued earth tones enrich a composite of white provincial cabinetry, oak flooring and space-efficient metal appliances.

French doors open the forward flex room to the front of the property—inviting an easy conversion to an office or guest space. Stone floors and recessed lighting effectively mingle past and present.

A gallery hall links the public rooms to a vestibule designed to maintain the privacy of the master retreat. Secluded from the secondary sleeping quarters, the owners' bedroom takes in wide ocean views and provides private access to the magnificent outdoor amenities of the rear yard.

harsh afternoon rays and glare, and eases the transition from the primary gathering space to the outdoors. The main gallery grants extensive vistas through the courtyard to the rear property, though the whole house is not obvious from the entry. Strategies evolved in the organization of the interior permit a progression of spaces. Linked by a *promenade architecturale*, the living and entertaining areas frame the open courtyard—a wonderful outdoor living space designed for casual meals and conversation. Positioned to enhance the visual aesthetic from every side, the courtyard fills the home with natural light and provides an optimal sense of space.

Primed with elements of the Early California vernacular, the rear elevation integrates Mission details with a catalog of Spanish Colonial influences. Designed to capture spectacular ocean views, the footprint faces the southwest and leads to an extended pool and spa area via a covered loggia.

Windward at Crystal Cove

LOCATION: NEWPORT BEACH, CALIFORNIA
BUILDER: RICHMOND AMERICAN

PHOTOGRAPHY: ERIC FIGGE 2001

3,865 SQUARE FEET

An ordered architecture primed with revival elements creates a sense of unity in a street scene keyed to subtle formulas of Old World and modern. Half walls and walkways visually define the entry courtyard and provide an invitation to neighboring.

Windward at Crystal Cove ┊ Nested in an exclusive community overlooking the sea at Crystal Cove, this Santa Barbara-style elevation engages Early California and Andalusian themes to establish its individual character. Subdued hues temper a gentle mix of past and present, integrating historic elements with a tapestry of American influences. Carefully designed to fit a slender coastal lot, the plan invests a straightforward façade with a refined Mediterranean dialect that is most simpatico with a relaxed waterside environment. With the quiet elegance of a rustic villa, this calm geometry of shapes suits its California hillside location, suggesting an architecture that is equally at home in the rolling hills of southern Spain.

Prominent features of the rear elevation—a covered loggia and upper-level deck—share their place in the sun with a grand turret. Rows of recessed windows offer views and light to the morning nook and upper-level master suite, while French doors permit indoor and outdoor spaces to mingle.

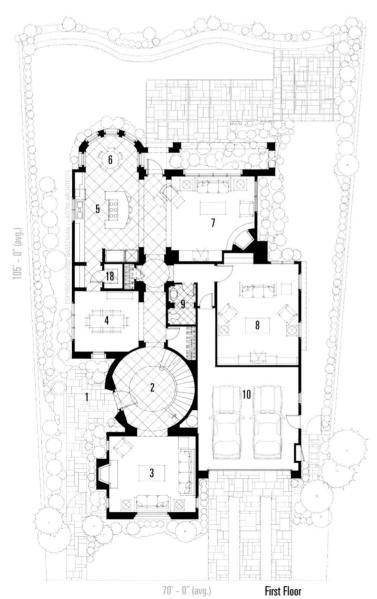

105' - 0" (avg.)

70' - 0" (avg.)   **First Floor**

1 Entry Courtyard
2 Entry
3 Living Room
4 Dining Room
5 Kitchen
6 Nook
7 Family Room
8 Media Room/Tandem Garage
9 Powder Room
10 Garage
11 Master Suite
12 Master Bathroom
13 Deck
14 Bedroom
15 Bathroom
16 Study Area
17 Laundry
18 Butler's Pantry

Second Floor

Left: The relaxed flavor of Santa Barbara-style architecture mixes classical and Early California vernacular forms with a grand-scale living space. Built-in cabinetry and a massive fireplace frame the central window—a focal point that visually governs the axial symmetry of the front of the plan.

Opposite page: Daylight from a broad front window visually links the living room to a showcase foyer set off by an elegant, detailed stair railing. Mosaic tile enriches the stone flooring of the entry rotunda, brightened by daylight from a row of tall clerestory windows.

Right: Sculpted arches define an open arrangement of informal spaces, including the well-equipped kitchen, morning bay and family room. Innovative architecture allows room proportions to vary—creating a comfortable ambience—and orients the informal areas toward ocean views.

The master bath captures panoramic ocean views, claiming the bayed nook for a step-up spa tub. Separate lavatories permit privacy for two owners, while a knee-space vanity adjoins a vestibule leading to the dressing area. Stone flooring, built-in cabinetry and wrought-iron accents enrich this private space.

A grand entry turret achieves harmony with the forward gables—a robust mix of colonial and Moorish details set off by a magnificent arch above the primary window. Decorative tiles highlight the front steps, inviting guests through a spacious side courtyard to an artfully paneled leaded-glass entry. The vaulted foyer showcases a winding stair and elaborate wrought-iron railing forged with an authentic, early 18th-century pattern that is completely in touch with the present. The entry rotunda links a secluded living room with the central gallery hall—a dominant axis progressing through the public realm to the informal living areas. To take full advantage of the property, the casual space is oriented toward views of the Pacific, while the forward rooms face the side courtyard.

An optional media center on the main level offers ample wall and floor space for a home theater and comfortable seating. Wired for the 21st Century, the house is fully prepared for electronic systems that ease the functions of everyday living. Positioned at the end of a private hall, the space easily converts to a fourth bedroom, media room or a tandem garage.

A perfect retreat for the homeowner, the upper-level master suite captures prime views and permits access to a wide private deck through French doors. Simple, shallow coffers complement a raised-hearth fireplace and banco, which pay homage to the appealing simplicity of Early California style.

Windward at Crystal Cove | RESIDENCE THREE

LOCATION: NEWPORT BEACH, CALIFORNIA
BUILDER: RICHMOND AMERICAN

PHOTOGRAPHY: ERIC FIGGE 2001

3,780 SQUARE FEET

This neo-Mediterranean façade is tempered with an attractive patina evocative of well-established communities such as Pasadena and Santa Barbara. A balcony and wrought-iron balustrade, recessed windows, lantern lights and scalloped eaves reinforce connections to the rural settings of southern Spain.

Windward at Crystal Cove ⫶ A Moorish influence enriches the old-meets-new entry of this romantic Spanish Colonial Revival elevation, with eye-pleasing decorative tile that embraces a well-crafted paneled door. Built in an upscale community overlooking the Newport coast, the style and mood of the home convey a strong sense of history, suggested by a parabolic window, bell-tower chimney and wrought-iron balustrade. Fractured massing relieves the solid stucco façade, which incorporates a bevy of elements: a modified turret, shed and

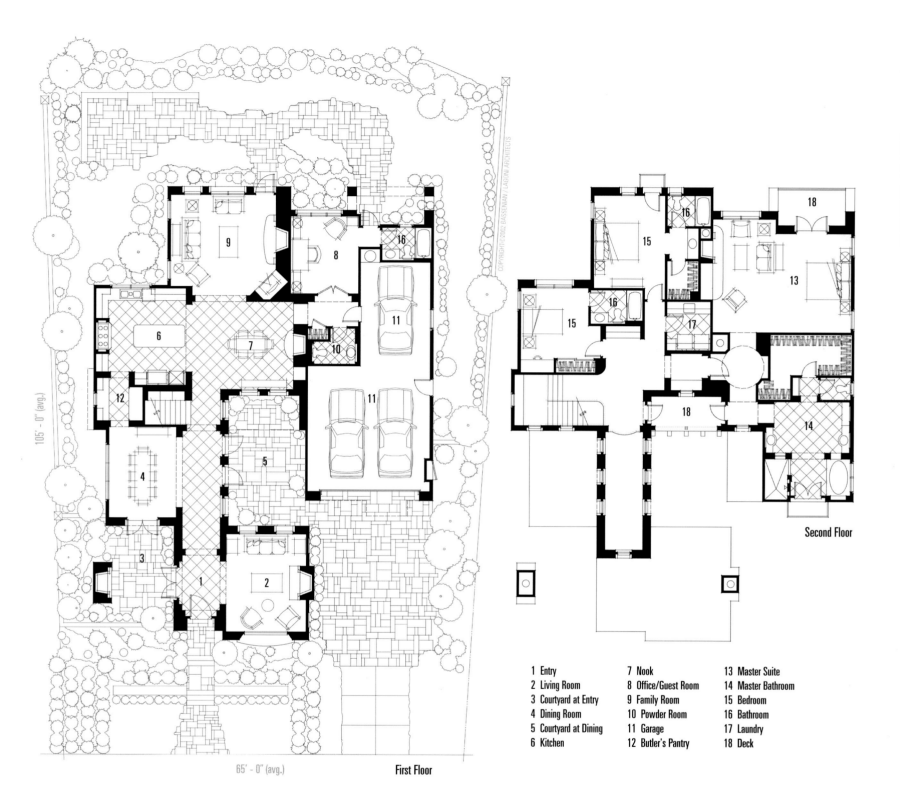

COPYRIGHT ©2002 BASSENIAN/LAGONI ARCHITECTS

105' - 0" (avg.)

65' - 0" (avg.)

First Floor

Second Floor

1 Entry	7 Nook	13 Master Suite
2 Living Room	8 Office/Guest Room	14 Master Bathroom
3 Courtyard at Entry	9 Family Room	15 Bedroom
4 Dining Room	10 Powder Room	16 Bathroom
5 Courtyard at Dining	11 Garage	17 Laundry
6 Kitchen	12 Butler's Pantry	18 Deck

gable rooflines, and layered wall surfaces. Just inside the foyer, French doors skillfully interpret the past with an immediate transition to the outdoors. Single- and two-story elements surround the entry courtyard, creating an intimate space that honors the style and grants natural light to the interior. A massive fireplace anchors the outer arena, adding another layer of authenticity to the Andalusian design. Between the vaulted foyer and the casual living areas, a second courtyard serves the architectural theme of the home and offers a place

of repose for its owners. Movement across the rear elevation permits various links to the outside, extending the informal areas while drawing in light and views. On the main level, flex-space options allow the plan to evolve to suit the owners' dynamic preferences. A den with a private entry is secluded to the rear of the plan, protected by the service vestibule and double interior doors—an inviting arrangement for a home office. With triple-window views and a nearby full bath and hall wardrobe, the room easily converts to guest quarters. A well-equipped kitchen and an interior nook with a raised fireplace give the home an edge over its period predecessors, capturing the earlier spirit of the region and enhancing it with a sense of luxury. Each of the formal rooms borders a separate courtyard—one a forward, intimate space and the other sprawling and relaxed—creating two distinct inside environments. The living room features a massive handcrafted fireplace and accepts refined views

Above: Dark wood surrounds and wrought-iron details maintain the character of rural Andalusian style in the morning nook, while a raised fireplace and banana-hued stucco provide a sense of contemporary luxury. A service hall to the left of the hearth leads to a secluded den or home office.

Right: Rustic elements—Euro cabinetry, a mosaic-tile backsplash and teak-toned hardwood floors—take on future-smart appliances in the gourmet kitchen. A butler's pantry positioned behind the stairway links the serving area to the formal dining room.

Below: Based on the architecture of southern Spain, the eclectic elevation takes on a closer massing at the rear of the plan—a pure interpretation of the style fitted with contemporary dimensions. The repetition of windows, wood surrounds and clay-tile roofs preserve the integrity and character of the Mediterranean influence.

Above: Seaside views dominate a refined décor in the casual living space, framed by bare stucco—a reference to the reformed Mission architecture discovered throughout the plan. The satisfying serenity of the space belies a system of advanced electronics and 21st-century media ware.

Oriented to the rear of the upper level, the master suite captures coastline views and opens to a private deck through French doors. A raised-hearth fireplace warms the sitting area of the owners' bedroom—a richly textured retreat that welcomes gentle ocean breezes.

from the inner courtyard. A broad archway, a triple-window view and French doors to the front courtyard inspire a relaxed atmosphere in the dining room. An interior balcony overlooks the dramatic two-story gallery foyer, which provides views of its own through rows of recessed clerestory windows. Expanded space at the landing offers a shared area for computers and books and leads to a forward deck. The orientation of the sleeping quarters to the rear of the plan achieves spectacular views for each bedroom, including a richly appointed master suite.

Windward at Crystal Cove : RESIDENCE FOUR

LOCATION: NEWPORT BEACH, CALIFORNIA
BUILDER: RICHMOND AMERICAN

PHOTOGRAPHY: ERIC FIGGE 2002

4,635 SQUARE FEET

An intimate courtyard merges a formal Andalusian-style paneled entry door with a more casual arena: an inviting outdoor space anchored by a fireplace with a sculpted stucco surround. The winding tile-clad staircase functions as a private entrance to an upper-level atelier or guest quarters.

Windward at Crystal Cove ⋮ Authentic stucco walls, recessed windows and rustic wrought-iron accents evoke the timeworn patina of an Early California villa, crafted with a vibrant contemporary approach to this revival style. Within a community of thirty-five homes nested in the Newport coastlands, this impressive four-bedroom plan conveys the requisite Santa Barbara theme in its exterior style, structure and ornamentation. Open spaces, hiking trails and serene walkways surround a hillside of eco-friendly lots throughout the neighborhood,

Secluded yet apparent to the street, the elevation offers a layered presentation from the sidewalk to the formal front entry. A gabled single-story element enhanced with graceful arches dominates the elevation and encloses the front courtyard.

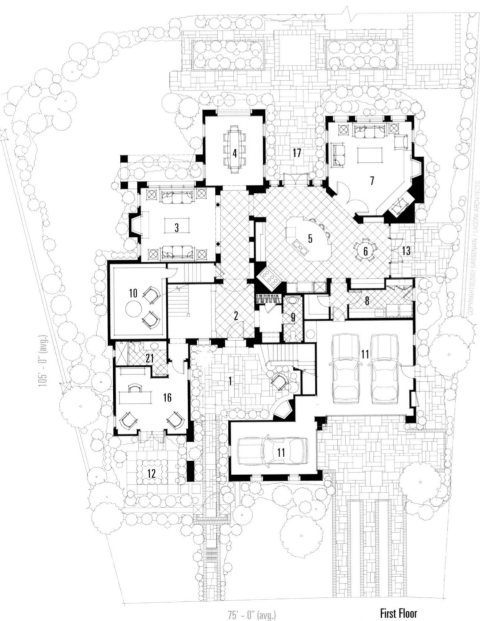

First Floor

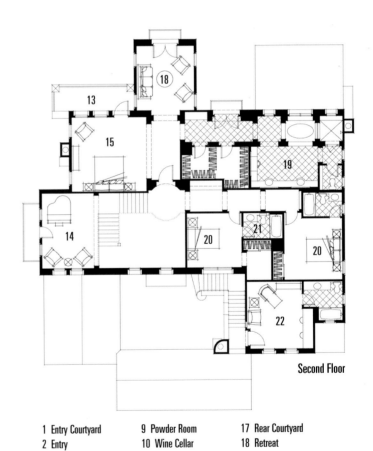

Second Floor

1 Entry Courtyard	9 Powder Room	17 Rear Courtyard
2 Entry	10 Wine Cellar	18 Retreat
3 Living Room	11 Garage	19 Master Bathroom
4 Dining Room	12 Front Courtyard	20 Bedroom
5 Kitchen	13 Deck	21 Bathroom
6 Nook	14 Library/Music Room	22 Studio/Guest Suite
7 Family Room	15 Master Suite	
8 Laundry	16 Office/Guest Room	

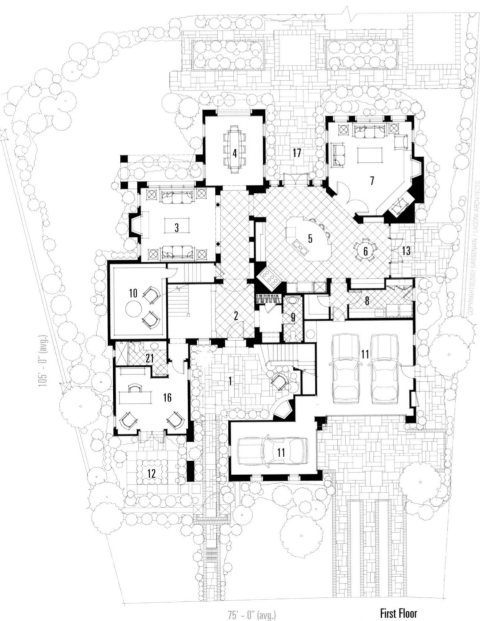

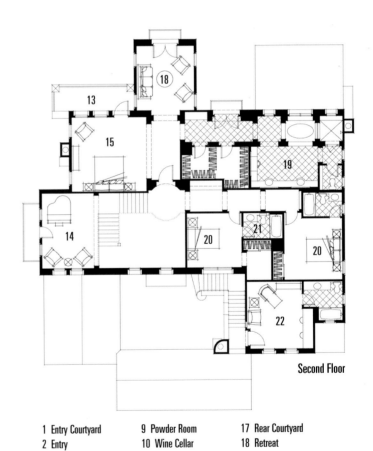

Hardwood accents and ivory paneled walls embrace a handcrafted staircase in the foyer. An intricate wrought-iron chandelier centers the magnificent two-story space and connects its modern ambience with the past. Built-in bookshelves line the gallery hall, which leads to the formal rooms.

Opposite page: A grand entry opens immediately to a two-story space—shaped by the mid-level library, a stepped railing and balcony overview. A sculpted archway leads directly ahead to the central gallery and provides access to the secluded wine cellar through a leaded-glass door.

encouraging an *at-home* relationship with the outdoors. A series of courtyards and outer areas on all sides of the house maintain the Spanish Colonial spirit and capture natural light and views. Across the width of the plan, a porte cochere appends the one-car garage to a broad single-story presentation that also encloses the front courtyard. An intimate and pristine area, the forecourt establishes a processional experience to the entry and provides private access to the optional studio or deck. Innovative forms and a soaring sculpted chimneystack add movement and heighten the visual excitement of the façade—a stucco-clad fractured elevation enhanced by arches and gables. The two-story entry ascends to the

library a half-level up—creating a private secondary formal space—
or leads through the gallery's sequence of arches to the dining
room. Rich with moldings and crafted panels, the formal rooms use
a balance of cool and warm colors to create serene spaces that
frame lavish views. A shallow coffer enhances the traditional living
room without departing from a relaxed and romantic Santa Barbara
theme that prevails throughout the home. On the other side of the
gallery hall, the casual living area orients an open arrangement of
the kitchen, nook and family room to the back property and coastal
views. Loggias, balconies and French doors allow inner and outside
spaces to intermingle.

*Below: Cool colors and a massive fireplace dominate the
living room, which provides ample views of the coastline
through a series of three windows. An open archway
links this space with the gallery and formal dining room.*

*Above: An open arrangement of the gourmet kitchen and
nook offers a spacious setting for informal gatherings
and casual meals. The island counter provides a snack
bar and overlooks a well-defined family room with wraparound views and a fireplace.*

*Opposite page: A picture window in the formal dining room
grants wide views of the Pacific Ocean and Newport coast.
The gallery hall permits the vista to extend to the foyer—
framed by the sculpted architecture of the interior.*

An optional studio or guest suite boasts private access through the entry courtyard and outer stairs. Complete with a full bath, built-in shelves and views of its own to the front property, the secluded space provides an opportunity to house a live-in relative.

Beyond the mid-level library, an upper-level entry vestibule leads to the spacious master suite—an unrestrained plan with lavish amenities and links to the outside. Walls of windows take in views of the Pacific and wrap the area with natural light. The owners' bedroom boasts a step-up retreat or sitting bay and a secluded deck. Two walk-in closets border a dressing area that introduces a bath with a perfectly framed whirlpool tub and a shower with a small recessed window to let in light. Designed for two owners, separate lavatories and a knee-space vanity grant even the most hectic lifestyles an aura of civility.

Below: The entry leads under the mid-level library to a stunning and spacious wine cellar through a leaded-glass door. Brick walls and floors provide a rich ambience dedicated to the quiet enjoyment of the homeowners' wine reserves.

Above: Carefully crafted to allow unobstructed ocean views, the terraced hillside sites also promote links to the outdoors for homeowners—with hiking trails and walkways woven into the community. The Spanish Colonial rear façade gracefully nestles into a space designed to optimize its coastal location.

Serena | RESIDENCE THREE

LOCATION: NEWPORT COAST, CALIFORNIA
BUILDER: SHEA HOMES

PHOTOGRAPHY: JEFFREY ARON 1999

3,696 SQUARE FEET

This Early California elevation steps boldly into the landscape, permitting panoramic views of the rugged foothills, coastline, canyons and city lights. With windows everywhere, even the formal spaces of this history house are light and open—complemented by a rambling interior that takes in daylight from every side.

Serena | Nested high above the Pacific near the coastlands of Newport Beach, the historic lines of this courtyard home convey the impressive artisanship of Early California architecture. With graceful sculpted forms punctuated by slender openings, the Spanish Colonial façade exhibits a subtle character influenced by the rugged architecture of a past era. Rough-hewn wood posts, exposed rafter tails, creamy stucco walls and low-pitched rooflines evoke an elemental Hispanic style, authenticated by cruciform ironworks and a primary parabolic window. A deeply carved Monterey-style balcony cantilevers above a main-level loggia, providing movement and depth to the façade and establishing an outdoor con-

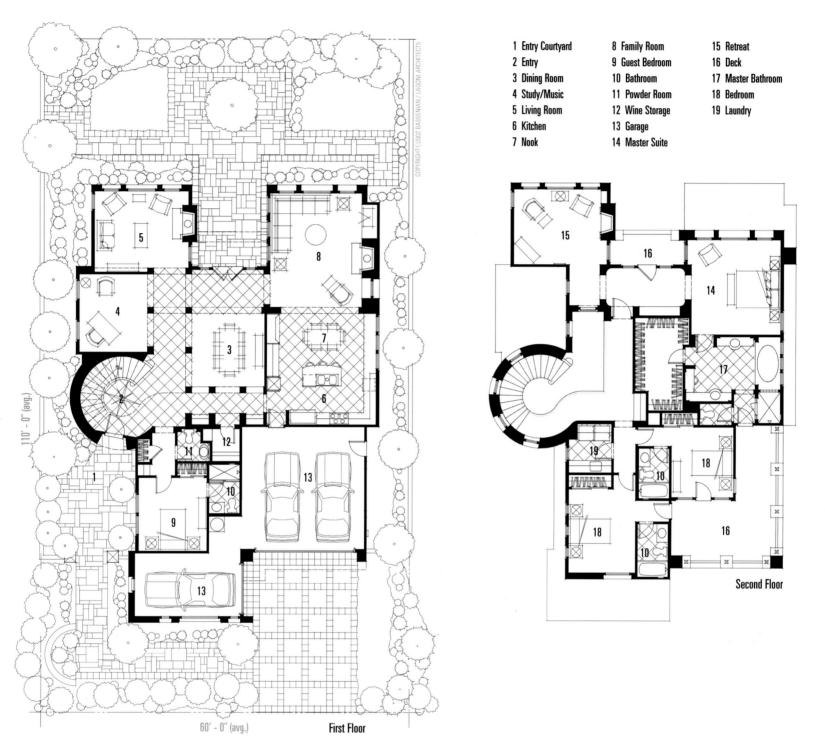

1 Entry Courtyard	8 Family Room	15 Retreat
2 Entry	9 Guest Bedroom	16 Deck
3 Dining Room	10 Bathroom	17 Master Bathroom
4 Study/Music	11 Powder Room	18 Bedroom
5 Living Room	12 Wine Storage	19 Laundry
6 Kitchen	13 Garage	
7 Nook	14 Master Suite	

110' - 0" (avg.)

60' - 0" (avg.)   **First Floor**

Second Floor

nection for the master suite. Set back from the street, the sculpted entry follows an informal progressive approach to the house through a well-landscaped courtyard. Positioned to the side of the plan, the grand turret plays counterpoint to the more playful, single-story element of the exterior, and provides vertical circulation within the foyer. An intricate entry sequence unfolds in two directions: toward the informal wing—past a vestibule that leads to a guest suite or home office—and toward the rear of the plan, terminating at the living room. The refined floor plan introduces airy outdoor spaces, such as the atrium, deck and front balcony, as well as many carefully defined places that provide wide views of the Newport

Designed to define the informal living space, a bow-arched soffit visually separates the family room from the tandem configuration of the gourmet kitchen and nook. Intimate gatherings and conversations about daily life center on the nook, which enjoys a primary position within the plan.

Coast. At the core of the plan, a colonnade wraps around the formal dining room, which opens to a rear-facing atrium. Informal spaces flow generously from one to another in an open-plan arrangement that employs the nook as a central gathering area. Flanked by a tandem configuration of the kitchen, nook and family room, the core creates a fluid relationship to the public realm and achieves the goal of bringing views to all of the primary living spaces on the main level. Glass walls line the rear elevation, capturing dramatic ocean views and visually extending the boundaries of the rooms.

Defined by a colonnade, the formal dining room takes in vistas and views from three sides. The open arrangement of public space provides circulation around the formal zone and visually expands the interior. Flat arches and detailed ironworks add texture to the space and maintain the colonial theme of the plan.

Somerton | RESIDENCE FOUR

LOCATION: IRVINE, CALIFORNIA
BUILDER: STANDARD PACIFIC HOMES

PHOTOGRAPHY: JOHN R. BARE 1999

3,344 SQUARE FEET

Rolling hills surround a two-story gable that serves as the focal point for the clean lines and clear California palette of a colonial elevation. An ornamented chimneystack plays counterpoint to close massing above the entry—relieved by a tall recessed window.

Somerton | Like an elegant villa that stands sentry to a vast estate, this high-end Irvine home steps into the landscape, sinking its historic roots into the lush scenery. An easy transition of spaces from the sidewalk to the entry of the Spanish Colonial façade creates a street-friendly approach to the house. Elements of the Early California vocabulary faithfully interpret the past: slender recessed windows, cantilevered rooflines and graceful archways. Through twin pilasters that guard the courtyard, a stone walkway proceeds to the paneled entry through an informal outdoor space and a covered loggia. A stunning spiral staircase highlights the dramatic, high-volume entry rotunda and provides an overlook from the upper gallery. On the main level, the central vestibule leads to an open arrangement of the formal rooms and spatially defines the casual living area through a deep square archway. Linked by a convenient butler's pantry, the dining room and gourmet kitchen take in plenty of daylight or moonlight—an inviting arrangement for traditional occasions. Placed just behind the stairwell, a spacious bedroom suite flexes to a den or home office. The upper-level sleeping quarters share a circular gallery hall that leads to a well-appointed master suite with a private fireplace. An adjoining bonus area converts to a recreation room.

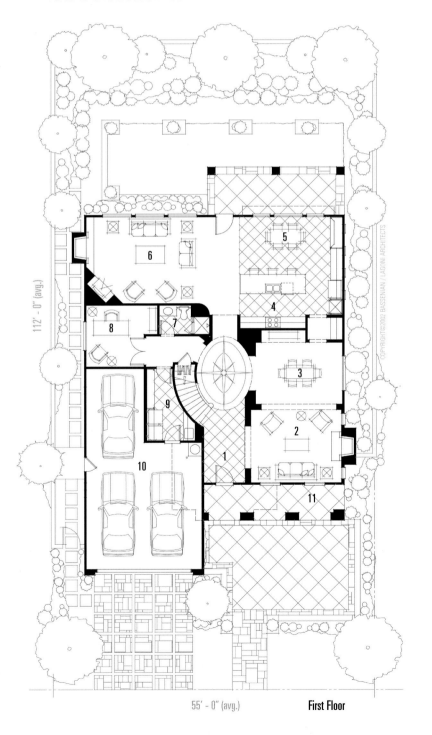

112' - 0" (avg.)

55' - 0" (avg.) **First Floor**

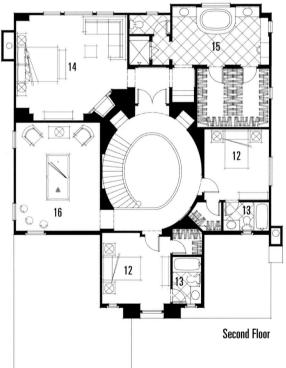

Second Floor

1 Entry	5 Nook	9 Laundry	13 Bathroom
2 Living Room	6 Family Room	10 Garage	14 Master Bedroom
3 Dining Room	7 Powder Room	11 Entry Porch	15 Master Bathroom
4 Kitchen	8 Home Office	12 Bedroom	16 Game Room

Montellano | RESIDENCE THREE

LOCATION: SAN CLEMENTE, CALIFORNIA
BUILDER: WILLIAM LYON HOMES

PHOTOGRAPHY: ERIC FIGGE 2002

4,695 SQUARE FEET

Montellano | Just shy of its centennial, San Clemente is the kind of old-new city that hosts year-round tours of one of California's earliest missions and boasts hot blues concerts on the sand in the summer. The mix seems deeply compatible in this place of breathtaking beauty—where fairways outnumber freeways and beach trains run the coast. Rich with history and rows of charming seaside cottages, the town accepts the authentic Spanish Colonial architecture of *Montellano* as an elemental piece of its vision. This home's white stucco walls and varied tile roofs embrace a circular tower and stately square chimneys. Ceramic and ironwork details articulate the Early California vocabulary, creating a fully stated street presence. A winding walkway leads to the paneled entry door and rotunda, which introduce an inviting interior embracing two central outdoor spaces: an open courtyard and a spacious

Above: Fractured massing creates a refined palette of intriguing angles and lines, displaying a colonial character that's both bold and contemporary. Clear blue skies and miles of ocean provide an idyllic backdrop for the white walls and red-tile roofs of the Early California vernacular.

Opposite page: The interior of the house embraces two central courtyards—one covered and one open—separated by a massive through-fireplace. (Top) A wide-open outdoor space features a Mexican saltillo tile floor and allows access from the den and the entry rotunda. (Bottom) Rustic furnishings flavor the theme of the covered patio and radiate from a focal-point fireplace, enhanced by a mosaic-tile surround.

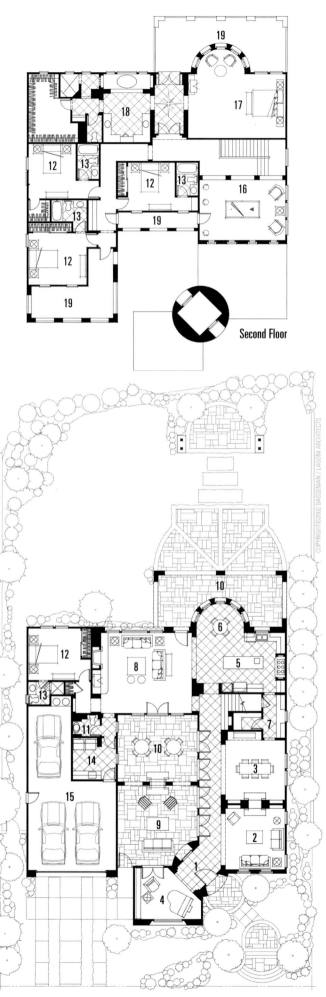

Second Floor

105' - 0" (avg.)

COPYRIGHT ©2002 BASSENIAN / LAGONI ARCHITECTS

60' - 0" (avg.)   **First Floor**

1   Entry

2   Living Room

3   Dining Room

4   Office/Music Room

5   Kitchen

6   Nook

7   Butler's Pantry

8   Family Room

9   Open Courtyard

10   Covered Courtyard/Patio

11   Powder Room

12   Bedroom

13   Bathroom

14   Laundry

15   Garage

16   Game Room

17   Master Suite

18   Master Bathroom

19   Desk

A bay window brightens the owners' retreat, allowing views and light to mingle. Luxurious furnishings enrich subdued décor, framing spectacular views in the bedroom. The central vestibule leads to a private deck and to the master bath, which provides separate vanities and a walk-in closet designed for two.

covered patio. Linked by a through-fireplace, the outside areas bring in natural light and allow fresh sea breezes and the temperate California climate to penetrate the house. The gallery hall provides a dramatic vista that extends beyond the morning bay to the back property. A staircase placed between the public and informal zones leads to the upper-level sleeping quarters, including a spectacular master suite. A private den at the front of the plan complements a flexible fifth bedroom that offers access from the family room or via the service entrance.

Elegant coffered ceilings highlight the formal rooms. Neutral tones complement luxurious furnishings in the living room, which is open to the entry and central gallery hall. A through-fireplace connects this space to the formal dining room.

A fireplace with a stucco surround shares the media wall with a built-in entertainment center in the family room. Floor-to-ceiling windows bring in a sense of nature, while a single door grants access to the outside. Nearby, the kitchen provides a snack counter and wide views of its own.

Right: Interior vistas extend the living room beyond its intimate boundaries and include the raised-panel entry door and spiral staircase. Tall twin windows offer outdoor views, which frame a discreet fireplace with a sculpted hood and polished mantel.

Opposite page: Curved, gravity-defying elements soar among the vaulted spaces of the foyer, emphasizing the drama of the home and enhancing the arrival experience. An open arrangement of the formal zone allows the full width of the house to be experienced at the rotunda.

Right: A series of broad soffits adds dimension and texture to the elegant formal dining room—crowned by a coffered ceiling. French doors open to a private patio, establishing an outdoor link that visually expands the space and brings in a sense of nature.

Wide windows frame the spacious family room, providing natural light that mingles with a relaxed décor and the crackle of a wood-burning fireplace. Generous dimensions permit a full media wall to enhance the informal gathering area of the home, inviting impromptu at-home theatre nights.

Distinctive pilasters and wrought-iron rails define the broad balcony of the rear elevation—underscoring rustic Spanish Colonial themes established at the streetscape. A French door provides access from the informal living area to a covered loggia and to a pool and spa.

A central food-preparation island in the gourmet kitchen features a snack counter with bar seating for easy meals—a perfect complement to the casual dining space provided by the morning nook. The curve of the bow window wraps the space with natural light and echoes the sculpted forms of the entry and foyer.

style tub, bringing spectacular views to dual vanity and dressing areas. The home's affinity for the great outdoors belies an innovative interior, which combines energy efficiency and resource conservation with high-end technology. Sited toward the panoramic views offered by the rear of the plan, the casual living area integrates high-end electronics with smart, eco-sensitive options: photo-selective glass, energy-saving appliances and a discreet recycling center hidden in the kitchen's cabinetry. Generous windows bring plenty of daylight into the family room, which features an elegant wood-burning fireplace and expansive views of the rolling terrain. Part of an advanced series with an unprecedented level of *green* building components, this highly livable plan links a healthy indoor environment with earth-smart features, including solar electricity.

Silver Creek : RESIDENCE TWO

LOCATION: COTO DE CAZA, CALIFORNIA
BUILDER: LENNAR HOMES

PHOTOGRAPHY: JOHN R. BARE 2002

The separation of two garages reduces the forward massing and maintains the simplicity of the building forms. A wraparound deck framed by dual balconies with wrought-iron details defines an inner courtyard. A recessed entry reiterates the layering of the façade, articulated by the extension of a low-pitched gable above the two-car garage.

Silver Creek ⋮ A Monterey-inspired Early California style that pays homage to the highly celebrated work of Wallace Neff, this romantic courtyard home evokes Old World architectural themes prevalent in the early 20th Century. Large, simple planes of white stucco punctuated by recesses, slender windows and a wraparound balcony authenticate the historic approach and satisfy the streetscape aesthetics of the gated community of Coto de Caza. Sited in a neighborhood patterned with equestrian trails and walkways, the simplicity of the elevation is a natural reference to its eco-friendly surroundings and to Neff's popular interpretations of the Spanish Colonial vernacular. Low-pitched rooflines and exposed clay-tile gable ends further delineate the style and define the inner courtyard, drawing the eye to the sculpted archway that precedes the entry. A high-volume vestibule increases circulation at the front of the home and allows the formal rooms to share spectacular outdoor views. The formal entry organizes the floor plan on a cross-axis that radiates from the living room. The "L" configuration stretches the perimeter of the home, allowing rooms throughout the interior to open to the outside spaces. An extension of the central gallery harbors the staircase, which is de-emphasized in order to pronounce the grandeur of the foyer. Upstairs, the gen-

A graceful balcony set off by wood balustrades celebrates the entrance to this Monterey-inspired elevation. Asymmetrical lines offer a vibrant interpretation of the early 20th-century style.

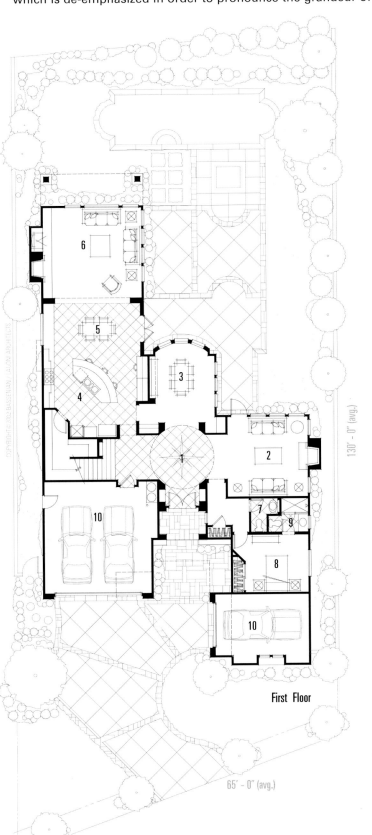

First Floor

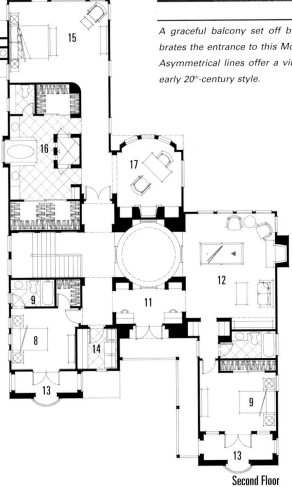

Second Floor

1 Entry
2 Living Room
3 Dining Room
4 Kitchen
5 Nook
6 Family Room
7 Powder Room
8 Bedroom
9 Bathroom
10 Garage
11 Study Area
12 Game Room
13 Deck
14 Laundry
15 Master Suite
16 Master Bathroom
17 Master Retreat

Left: An upper-level gallery overlooking the entry speaks volumes about the arrangement of inner space. The abstract placement of geometrical shapes creates the illusion of the gallery floating above the main level. Negative and positive forms softened by indirect lighting enrich the sculpted environment, adding dimension and texture to the open arena.

Opposite page: A vaulted entry chamber introduces the drama and grandeur of the home and allows interior vistas to extend the boundaries of the public rooms. Soaring curved forms temper the dominant vertical lines that frame the living room, which opens to the right of the entry. The formal dining room adjoins the circular vestibule and offers grand outdoor views through a bay window.

Right: A flat arch defines open space between the family room and the morning nook and kitchen. Spectacular views embrace this informal area, bringing in natural light and a sense of the outdoors. A square archway to the left of the appliance wall connects the food preparation and serving area to the dining room through a butler's pantry.

erous dimensions of the master suite create a lavish comfort zone for the homeowners. A private entry vestibule leads to a separate retreat and to a gallery that links the well-appointed bath with the owners' bedroom. Built-in desks frame a study area in the upper-level hall, which connects the secondary bedroom suites and opens to the forward wraparound deck. The allocation of open space around the balcony overlook, study area and bonus room assigns an individual character to the area and underscores the creative spirit of the home.

Heritage Walk

LOCATION: PASADENA, CALIFORNIA
BUILDER: THE OLSON COMPANY

PHOTOGRAPHY: ERIC FIGGE 2000

1,191 TO 1,785 SQUARE FEET

Distinctive forms and the varied treatment of separate entries have drawn high praise for the Mission-inspired façade. The new multi-family project provides an in-town living environment for couples and noncommuters—who have the opportunity to walk to restaurants, theaters and historic sites.

Heritage Walk | Within walking distance of the progressive heart of Pasadena, this in-town community of thirty-eight attached homes gently mixes cyber-oriented interiors with an artful interpretation of the Early California vernacular. Well recognized for its preservation of historic landmarks and the vibrant revitalization of its business district, Pasadena is a city that requires residential designers to hit the nail squarely on the head when mapping out a piece of its streetscape. A remarkable fusion of urban substance and Hispanic style, this new multi-family development achieves an authentic character that honors the fiber of the community with a highly cultivated design. Recognized with numerous awards, *Heritage Walk* offers a distinctive Mission-style architecture reflecting an amalgam of regional influences— inspired by the signature structures of a famous city with a significant cultural heritage. In another time, its innovative beauty and cordial relationship to the street would have easily

Left: Varied massing and separate roof forms highlight the striking rear elevation. A configuration of three- and four-story building masses create a layered appearance and allow prominent mountain views inside. The sculpted archway provides access to the homeowners' private attached garages.

Below: Residence Two features a versatile third bedroom that easily converts to a studio or a convenient home office. The lower level provides a stair hall, nearby storage and direct access to an attached private two-car garage.

Right: Perched on the third and fourth floors of the building's prominent corner towers, Residence Three offers a spacious living area and wide views of the San Gabriel Mountains. Daylight brightens an elegant dining room that leads to a private deck.

qualified the project as a good urban neighbor. Sited in the commuter district of a fast-paced, live/work environment, though, the savory presentation and compelling aesthetics of this infill community are forced to be a mere introduction to its work-savvy, flexible interiors. Well suited for the lifestyles of city dwellers and young professionals, the individual houses combine many of the elements of a traditional town home: a private entry, multi-level living options and an attached garage. Combinations of three- and four-story units, ranging in size from 1,191 to 1,785 square feet, offer two or three bedrooms, two or three baths, and a one- or two-car garage with direct access to each unit.

Chapter Two

CALIFORNIA TUSCAN HOMES

Brilliant sunflowers and Renaissance frescoes somehow go together in Tuscany. Doric porticos and rough-hewn walls, ghosts of grand dukes and families of *butteri*—cowboys who herd wild horses on meadows by the sea—live in harmony there. Deeply carved valleys lead to jagged coastal cliffs in this colorful ancient land—known best, perhaps, for its sun-drenched hillsides and sprawling villas. A Tuscan house improves with age. The land confers a dignity upon its rustic walls, synchronizing intractable rhythms of stone and stucco, ochre and sky-blue. Ancient and modern elements come together in the Tuscan-inspired designs on the next few pages. Highly textured stucco walls awash with saturated sienna hues, detailed ironworks and rugged planked entries evoke the native charm of centuries-old manors. Open galleries with massive fireplaces, serene courtyards, sculpted arcades and rambling terraces address their surroundings with a 21st-century spirit. Authentic temperaments glide into contemporary spaces, integrate seamlessly with *today* lifestyles and offer sanctuary, even in the heart of the city.

Villas at The Bridges | RESIDENCE ONE

LOCATION: RANCHO SANTA FE, CALIFORNIA
BUILDER: HCC INVESTORS/LENNAR COMMUNITIES

PHOTOGRAPHY: ERIC FIGGE 2002

3,104 SQUARE FEET

1 Entry Courtyard

2 Entry

3 Great Room

4 Kitchen

5 Morning Room

6 Master Suite

7 Master Bathroom

8 Loggia

9 Bedroom

10 Bathroom

11 Home Office

12 Powder Room

13 Casita

14 Media Room/Opt. Dining Room

15 Laundry

16 Garage

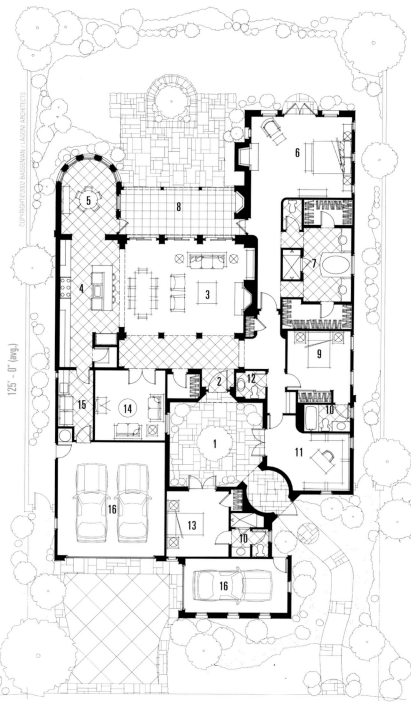

125' - 0" (avg.)

65' - 0" (avg.)

COPYRIGHT ©2002 BASSENIAN | LAGONI ARCHITECTS

Above: Rough stone and smooth, contrasting stucco enjoy a definite connection to the Tuscan region, replicating the open galleries, enormous fireplaces and thick stone walls of old Tuscan farmhouses.

Opposite page: Like a door within a door, a rough-hewn timber gate grants entrance to a quiet courtyard through a massive stone propylaeum. The open inner arena offers a pleasant procession from the courtyard to the formal entry.

Villas at The Bridges Well adapted to the gently rolling terrain of *The Bridges at Rancho Santa Fe*—a California community encompassing a spectacular golf course—this Tuscan-inspired courtyard home is sited toward the fairway with stream and hillside views. A magnificent gated entrance, situated in opposition to the front- and side-loading garages, provides a processional experience through an inner courtyard to a formal front entry—intimating a *postigo*, or door within a door. True to Tuscan style, a variety of spaces unfold radially from the courtyard, granting private access to a guest bedroom and a home office. The tiled foyer presents a stimulating visual experience, allowing the plan to progress gradually from the central gallery. Living spaces are airy: clerestory windows and French doors are employed to extend indoor spaces beyond the limits of the rooms. The house mixes wide-open views with various details such as recessed lighting, coffered ceilings, robust square arches and exposed timber trusses. Massive stone fireplaces create com-

Above: Ribbon windows surround a sunlit morning room, highlighted by rustic timber beams—a reference to the rural vernacular of the Italian countryside. Juxtaposed with a modern chandelier and furnishings, the architecture seems timeless.

Opposite page: The massive chest-plank door and cast-stone surround of the arched entry complement a series of period windows. A beautifully proportioned courtyard establishes a sensible, pedestrian-scaled perimeter that eases the transition from the street.

fort zones inside and out, enriching comfortable décor and casually elegant furnishings. A pragmatic spirit prevails throughout the house: an open arrangement of the great room, kitchen and formal dining room invites planned events and eases everyday functions. The master suite is placed deep to the rear of the plan, lending expansive views to the owners' bedroom. A sheltered corridor creates a second courtyard with an exterior fireplace. The covered loggia features an exposed wood tongue-and-groove ceiling stained in deep sienna. Brick pavers create a traditional texture that extends to a grassy esplanade, inviting enjoyment of breezes and views.

Above: A bright, airy kitchen boasts up-to-date amenities and hand-painted tiles, enhanced by solid timber trusses and tall clerestory windows. Robust arches and vintage cabinetry invigorate subdued space-age culinary features, such as the sculpted ventilator hood.

Right: Ochre-colored stucco and rough stone embrace a rear covered loggia that serves as a second courtyard. Gable, rake and hip forms break down the elevation's mass to a comfortable scale.

Opposite page: A separate entry leads from the courtyard to the home office or library, granting access from the outside without violating the privacy of the house. Rugged and smooth textures woven together create a sense of intimacy, yet the room is grand.

Right: Dark wood floors enrich the homeowner's bedroom, decorated in an elegant style with cool, unpretentious furnishings. Multi-pane clerestory windows evocative of an established Tuscan villa surround French doors that bring in a sense of the outdoors.

Villas at The Bridges | RESIDENCE TWO

LOCATION: RANCHO SANTA FE, CALIFORNIA
BUILDER: HCC INVESTORS/LENNAR COMMUNITIES

PHOTOGRAPHY: ERIC FIGGE 2002

3,332 SQUARE FEET

Masonry and rough stone establish a sense of history within a footprint that appears to ramble yet is deliberately structured to enhance the house spatially. A linear façade takes on an individual character by rotating the angle of the garage, resulting in a space that functions as a prelude to the enclosed entry.

Villas at The Bridges | Situated above a luxuriant valley, this rustic elevation captures the character of a 15th-century Italian manor, expressing its individuality with an asymmetrical arrangement of forms. Heavily influenced by the centuries-old architecture of the rambling Tuscan countryside, the imposing masonry façade employs course-rubble gables and massive arches to establish its simple provenance. Tile-capped rooflines create a harmonious geometry dominated by a small stone tower, which helps to establish a refined presence in the gentle hills of Rancho Santa Fe. A peaceful spirit settles across the combination of shapes, arranged around two distinctive courtyards—a formal space near the turreted entry and a casual area encountered deeper in the plan. Announced by a gated portal, the fore-

Sited toward a magnificent fairway bordered by a fresh-water stream, the rear elevation and pergola create an outdoor environment that is designed for entertaining and communing with nature.

1 Entry Courtyard	7 Bedroom	13 Gallery Hall
2 Entry	8 Powder Room	14 Garage
3 Great Room	9 Second Master Suite	15 Loggia
4 Kitchen	10 Bathroom	16 Casita
5 Master Suite	11 Laundry	
6 Master Bathroom	12 Interior Courtyard	

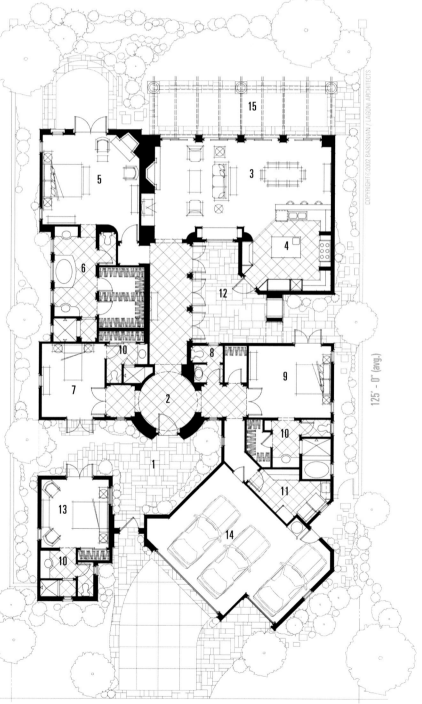

court creates a sense of privacy for the house and a wonderful exterior space for the *casita*, a detached dwelling that's easily converted to an office or guest suite. The prominent placement of the smaller house allows great views of the courtyard and access to the sun through French doors. Cast-iron elements add dimension and an Old World flavor to the rugged foyer—a tall, stone-clad entryway that leads in three directions to private and public realms. Opposing bedroom suites relate cross-axially to the central gallery hall, which links the primary and secondary sleeping quarters with an informal living space. Architectural details—exposed timber trusses that act as structural members—contribute in subtle and sophisticated ways to a spare, authentic décor that visually unifies the interior with its august exterior. Living spaces that flex from formal to casual reside at the rear of the plan, where a large expanse of glass provides unrestricted views and allows inside and outside areas to mingle. A high continuous band of clerestory windows syncopates the rhythm of

Above: Beams of natural light penetrate the sophisticated ambience of the great room, enriching the texture of the hardwood floors and exposed timber beams. Flexing from formal to casual, the combined living and dining space connects to the pergola through French doors.

Left: Rich with authentic details, such as exposed timber trusses and transom-level stone, the central gallery hall opens to a protected side courtyard. With a sitting area warmed by a massive hearth, the court functions as an outdoor living space that is accessed by public and private rooms.

Opposite page: An intimate entry court leads to a volume foyer within a stone turret—initiating a complex and purposeful visual experience that directs the eye upward as well as toward the linear space presented by the central gallery.

the trusses and relieves the solid masonry of the rear wall. Natural light brightens a palette of earth hues, leather furnishings and Eastern accents played against the ochre walls and wood floors, bringing an unexpected richness to the décor. Commercial-quality appliances provide a striking counterpoint to rough-hewn cabinetry, wrought-iron details and a massive stucco surround above the cooktop in the gourmet kitchen. An open dining room shares the warmth of the hearth, while glass doors to the covered loggia invite the possibility of meals alfresco. The rear of the house is remarkably open, revealing the architect's deep regard for nature and landscape. All of the French doors in the living area open to a pergola that stretches toward stunning views of the fairway, pond and stream.

Left: Stone and mosaic tile in the homeowners' bath enrich the décor and ground the design with a sense of permanence. Hardware, fixtures—even colors—were all carefully chosen to express the timelessness of the architecture.

Opposite page: A series of clerestory windows plays counterpoint to recessed lighting fixtures, casting an ambient glow on a rich palette of textures and tones in the open dining room and kitchen. Rough-hewn hardwood floors mix easily with modern culinary appliances to create an inviting space for events and gatherings.

Below: French doors open from the master bedroom to the outside—bringing in fresh air and spectacular views of the fairway and stream. A sun terrace invites the owners to enjoy the wide open spaces and native resources that surround the home.

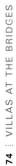

Villas at The Bridges RESIDENCE THREE

LOCATION: RANCHO SANTA FE, CALIFORNIA
BUILDER: HCC INVESTORS/LENNAR COMMUNITIES

PHOTOGRAPHY: ERIC FIGGE 2002   3,836 SQUARE FEET

Villas at The Bridges | Reminiscent of a 300-year-old Italian country villa, this Tuscan-inspired home explores the integration of romantic Old World and early California architecture. A glimpse through the gated front portal reveals a beautifully proportioned courtyard, framing a stone entry turret. Broad expanses of simple, highly textured exterior walls are sparingly articulated with neo-Romanesque forms, unified by rows of recessed windows. Two square chimneys evocative of mission bell towers enhance an arrangement of shed and hip clay-tile roofs, where rafter tails and corbels add period details to the eave lines. The home is entered

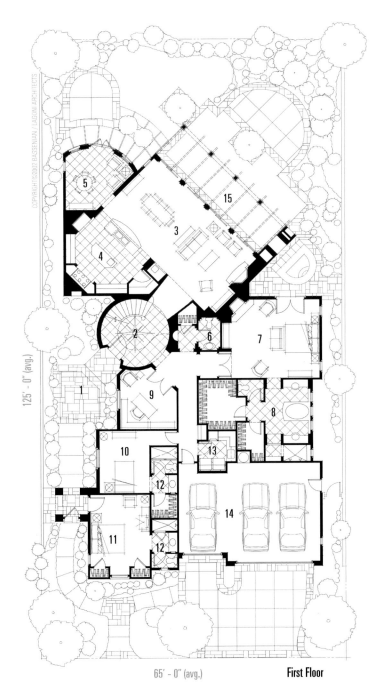

First Floor

65' - 0" (avg.)

125' - 0" (avg.)

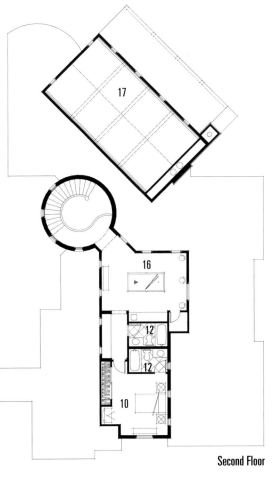

Second Floor

1 Entry Courtyard
2 Entry
3 Great Room
4 Kitchen
5 Morning Room
6 Powder Room
7 Master Suite
8 Master Bathroom
9 Office
10 Bedroom
11 Casita
12 Bathroom
13 Laundry
14 Garage
15 Loggia
16 Bonus Room
17 Volume over Great Room

Architectural stone, set off by exposed wood trusses, is placed strategically at the transom level above four sets of French doors in the dining and living area.

In the homeowners' bath, stone tiles line a jetted soaking tub framed by separate vanities and a dressing area leading to two walk-in closets.

through a deep foyer surrounding a turreted stair, which leads to an upper-level guest suite and game room. Glazed tiles and ornate wrought-iron quatrefoils in the double-height entry hall suggest a turn toward renaissance elements and introduce a refined interior to the relative informality and rugged character of the exterior. Pale honey-toned walls highlight a palette of earth hues that prevails beyond the entry. Interior vistas extend from the paneled front door to the rear loggia, providing a great sense of spaciousness and light. The house massing pivots 45 degrees at the rotunda, permitting spectacular views of the gently rolling landscape and golf course through the projecting bay. A sculpted barrel-vaulted opening leads into the main living area, which is bordered by four sets of French doors granting a strong visual connection to the outside. Heavy timber trusses and a massive cast-stone fireplace provide an authentic presence and texture to the space. A unique two-sided outdoor fireplace is situated to the rear of the loggia, also warming a private enclave that opens from the master bedroom.

Honey-toned stucco, rough-faced stones and clay-tile roofs celebrate their splendid settings in Southern California, where—as in Tuscany—life is focused as much on outdoor as indoor spaces.

Serena : RESIDENCE TWO

LOCATION: NEWPORT COAST, CALIFORNIA
BUILDER: SHEA HOMES

PHOTOGRAPHY: JEFFREY ARON 1999

3,692 SQUARE FEET

Saturated colors set off this historic yet perfectly contemporary home, enriched with romantic elements evocative of an Italian Country manor. True to its Tuscan roots, the plan's layered massing conveys the sense of an evolved elevation expanded over time. Subtle forms and authentic details express the nature of a discreet hillside villa.

Serena : This Tuscany-inspired exterior features a sculpted entry preceded by an Old World courtyard and framed by single-story gables replete with stone accents. Varied low-pitched rooflines and vertical proportions establish a comfortable scale for the elevation—which exhibits Italian Country elements, such as tilt-turn louvered shutters and a wrought-iron balcony. The forecourt grants access through French doors to a well-positioned home office or fourth bedroom tucked behind the single-car garage. Beyond the paneled entry door, a high-volume circular foyer functions as a vestibule that directs flow axially to a flex space and forward to a gallery hall. Defined by a series of arches, the prominent corridor extends the

From its vantage point overlooking the ocean, Newport Harbor and the surrounding coastlands, the four-sided architecture of this coastal villa allows the California climate inside. Layered surfaces, notched courtyards, decks and covered porticos break up the massing and lend texture to the elevation. Large windows bring light and gentle breezes to the interior.

1 Entry Courtyard
2 Entry
3 Living Room
4 Dining Room
5 Kitchen
6 Nook
7 Family Room
8 Wine Cellar
9 Powder Room
10 Office/Guest Room
11 Bathroom
12 Laundry
13 Garage
14 Master Suite
15 Master Bathroom
16 Deck
17 Study
18 Bedroom

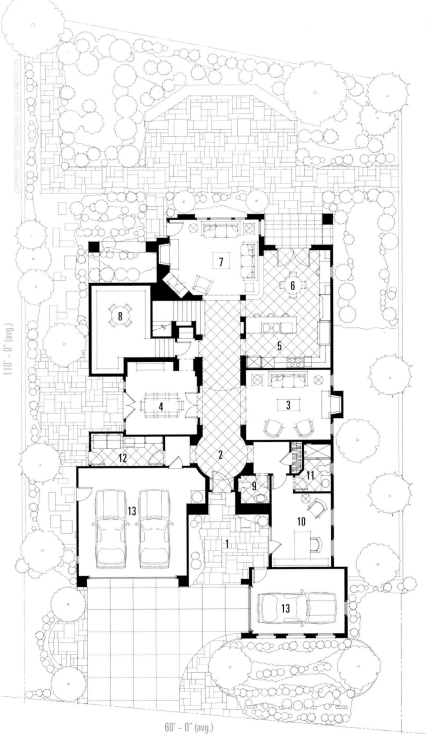

110' - 0" (avg.)

60' - 0" (avg.)

First Floor

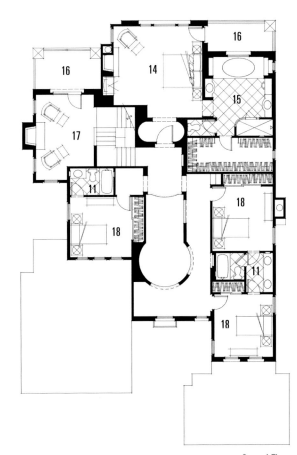

Second Floor

Below: Rich European wood cabinetry warms the ambience of the gourmet kitchen. A food preparation island provides a vegetable sink and shares space with an extensive snack counter. Stainless steel culinary appliances complement the new-age Old World look.

Above: Contemporary lines in the morning nook play counterpoint to the relaxed, more rural, theme of the exterior. A half-wall permits interior vistas, enriched by the rugged stone surround on the fireplace in the adjoining family room.

A varied palette enriches the living room, which includes an impressive cast-stone fireplace. Paneled walls and recessed lighting add dimension and texture to the space, which opens through an archway from the central gallery hall. Directly opposed to the formal dining room, the living space shares natural light from the side courtyard.

plan's sight lines to the family room, where tall windows frame views of the Pacific. A restrained floor plan allows a careful sequence of spaces to unfold progressively— optimizing the multi-dimensional visual experience. Tall windows and French doors in the formal rooms and casual living areas maximize the benefits of the coastal location and moderate climate. Notched courtyards bring in natural light and ocean breezes at the dining room and nook. Midway to the upper level, an office or den enjoys a private deck and seclusion from the primary living areas and sleeping quarters. Tucked below this mid-level room is a storage space that flexes to a private wine cellar. On the upper level, the master suite takes advantage of its placement across the full plan width and boasts its own fireplace, a private deck and an inviting entry vestibule. A balcony overlook to the foyer separates two bedroom suites and an optional fifth bedroom.

Placed below the mid-level den, the wine cellar provides an intimate tasting area and ample controlled storage. A privacy door leads to the butler's pantry, which links to the formal dining room and leads to the gourmet kitchen.

Tesoro Crest

LOCATION: NEWPORT COAST, CALIFORNIA
BUILDER: STANDARD PACIFIC

PHOTOGRAPHY: JOHN BARE 1998

Expressive details on the neighborhood-friendly façade transmit a sense of tradition attuned to the disposition of a European hill town by the sea. A secondary suite with a forward deck cantilevers over a home office converted from flex space.

Tesoro Crest | Situated on a slender lot above the Newport coast, this rustic Mediterranean manor basks in an eclectic mix of Euro elements—primarily Tuscan with simultaneous Norman influences. Varied rooflines and asymmetrical cross gables convey a fractured, non-monolithic approach to the elevation. Tall windows, quaint shutters, cavetto-style moldings, decorative corbels and stone accents further break the scale of the façade, evoking the charm of Old World country houses that were expanded over time. Interior vistas extend axially from the tiled entry to the formal zone, extending the sight lines beyond the rear of the plan. Side-by-side formal and casual living spaces share an orientation toward wide ocean views.

Floor-to-ceiling windows frame ocean views that enhance the formal area of the interior. French doors lead to an entertainment terrace that adjoins a sheltered outside space accessed from the family room.

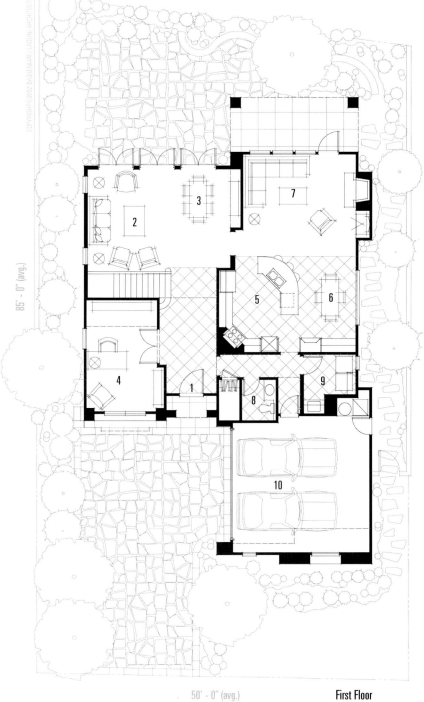

85' - 0" (avg.)

50' - 0" (avg.)

First Floor

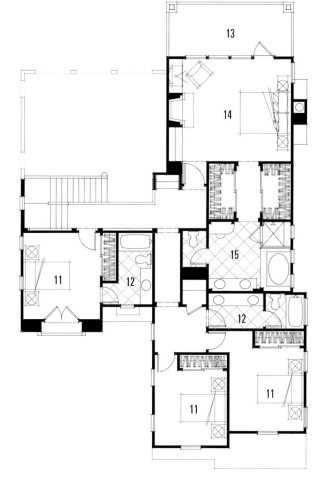

Second Floor

1 Entry	6 Nook	11 Bedroom
2 Living Room	7 Family Room	12 Bathroom
3 Dining Room	8 Powder Room	13 Deck
4 Home Office	9 Laundry	14 Master Suite
5 Kitchen	10 Garage	15 Master Bath

Triana : RESIDENCE TWO

LOCATION: ESCONDIDO, CALIFORNIA
BUILDER: HEARTHSIDE HOMES

PHOTOGRAPHY: JEFFREY ARON 2000

2,587 SQUARE FEET

Rich, saturated hues add life to the streetscape and link the layered façade to its Tuscan roots. A fresh interpretation of neo-Mediterranean style, the house is a vehicle for exploration, with clever allocations of space that defy tradition and ease everyday functions.

Triana : The softly rolling hills of San Pasqual shelter this Escondido community of stunning Old World homes, surrounded by 700 acres of park and wilderness. Sited on a lush hilltop rich with age-old oak trees, this Tuscan-style home overlooks a secluded valley and commands magnificent views of the region. Variety in form and style are the architectural keynotes of this neighborhood, which offers three distinct European Country styles. A bold turret integrates the fractured two-story form of this Tuscan elevation, while side gables and a varied roofline reduce the massing and permit a layered appearance. An open arrangement of the entry rotunda, living room and home office provides a space that easily flexes to facilitate planned events as well as the office hours of noncommuters. Clerestory windows above the stairs provide plenty of natural light for a computer loft that is large enough for more than one child to work independently.

Honey-toned cabinetry and smooth, shiny surfaces surround a well-equipped food preparation space in the gourmet kitchen. The nook provides an easy place for casual meals and provides access to a covered loggia. Behind the nook, a graceful archway leads to the formal dining room through a butler's pantry.

The living room provides a comfortable formal environment, enhanced by wide views of the luxuriant scenery. Open to the vaulted entry and the den or office, the combined space easily converts from a business environment to an entertainment area. Secluded from the informal zone, the office allows clients to come and go without disturbing the everyday pace of the household.

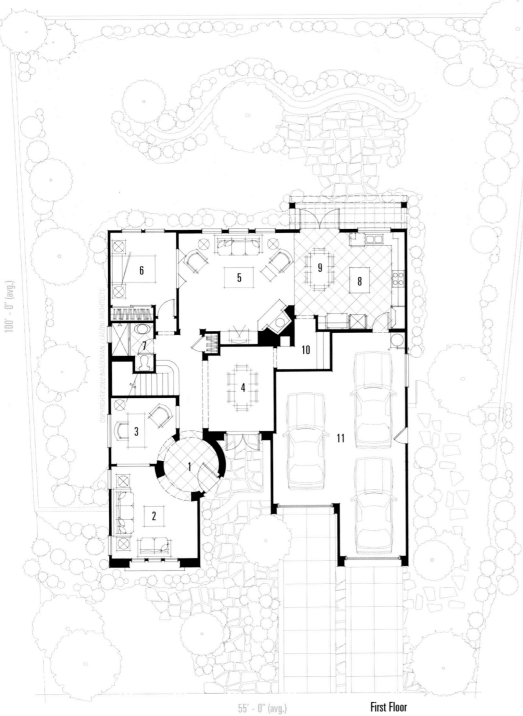

100' - 0" (avg.)

55' - 0" (avg.)   First Floor

Second Floor

1 Entry	7 Powder Room	13 Master Suite
2 Living Room	8 Kitchen	14 Master Bathroom
3 Den/Office	9 Nook	15 Bathroom
4 Dining Room	10 Butler's Pantry	16 Laundry
5 Family Room	11 Garage	17 Deck
6 Bedroom	12 Study Area	

Chapter Three

CALIFORNIA COASTAL HOMES

These days, people can plant roots just about anywhere. We plug into a vast virtual realm as easily as we pick up a phone, and our worldwide ability to connect to cyberspace has changed nearly everything. Finding home in the West's coastal regions is an intriguing venture that could lead to a beachy Bungalow at water's edge or a vintage seaboard cottage in a familiar neighborhood—a cliffside pied-a-terre or an untamed masterpiece on the far outside. Powerful forms meld with the quiet palettes of seaside communities without apology, shaping a diverse architecture that responds to the rare California climate with bold montages of glass, steel and stone. More than any other vernacular, the coastal style plays out the spirit of the region, the unlike-any-other feel of the place, with homes that are both historic and future-friendly. Evolved designs on these pages absorb the scenery and flex to live-work schedules, hug the shore and provide hip shelter—they are real-world houses that nobly confront the ocean with new notions of *home*.

Laguna Beach Residence

LOCATION: LAGUNA BEACH, CALIFORNIA
BUILDER: AKINS CONSTRUCTION

PHOTOGRAPHY: JOHN R. BARE 1997

5,726 SQUARE FEET

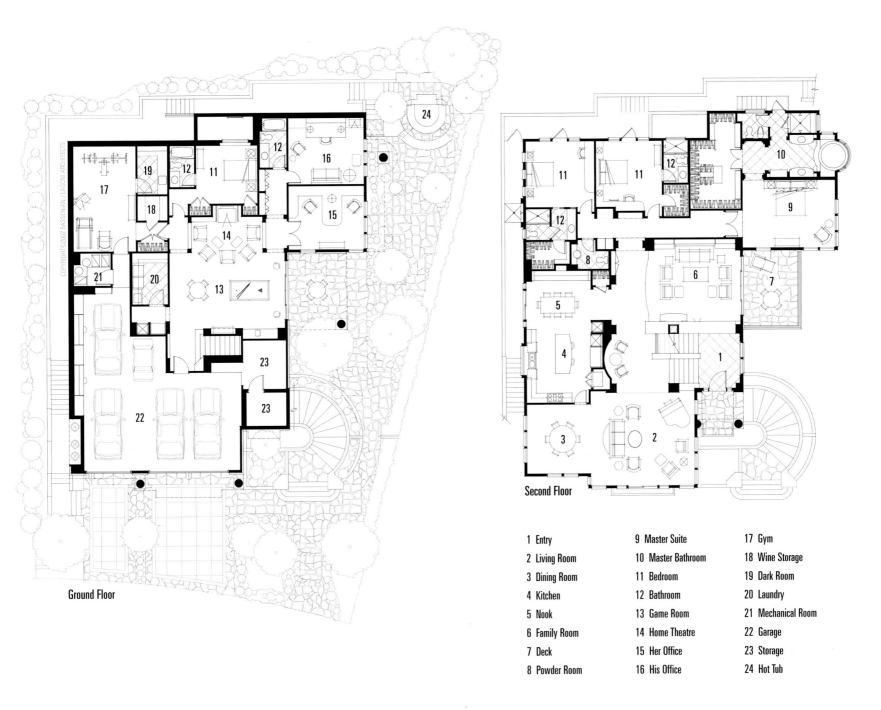

Ground Floor

Second Floor

COPYRIGHT©2002 BASSENIAN / LAGONI ARCHITECTS

1 Entry	9 Master Suite	17 Gym
2 Living Room	10 Master Bathroom	18 Wine Storage
3 Dining Room	11 Bedroom	19 Dark Room
4 Kitchen	12 Bathroom	20 Laundry
5 Nook	13 Game Room	21 Mechanical Room
6 Family Room	14 Home Theatre	22 Garage
7 Deck	15 Her Office	23 Storage
8 Powder Room	16 His Office	24 Hot Tub

Opposite page: A tribute to the architect's invention, the house expresses both the climate and context of its surroundings. Imaginative and playful, the home embodies visional architecture yet the rugged structure is fully prepared for the coastal elements. The plan flows easily toward western views and permits plenty of daylight through the south walls.

Laguna Beach Residence A southern California architect's private residence, this cutting-edge design carves an elegant profile in the hills above the quiet, scenic community of Laguna Beach. A high-energy exterior oxygenates the streetscape with a beachy East-meets-West aesthetic that emphasizes its idyllic location. Set high above the coastline, the dramatic elevation displays an uninhibited spirit suited to the luxuriant canyons that surround it and claims a spectacular sea view that stretches for miles in each direction. Powerful forms shape the façade, reflecting the kind of design bravado that captivates the owner's clients and breathes fresh air into the stringent idioms of Eastern seaboard vernaculars—yet the

An unrestrained California interpretation of the Eastern seaboard vernacular fits its primary seaside location and the free-spirit style of the neighborhood. Graceful curves— on the forward soffit and the winding stair—bring the bold vertical proportions of the elevation into high relief.

house is a common-sense structure, an honest expression of the architect's dream. With all of its pure intentions, the home employs extraordinary measures to resolve the complexity of a restrictive, steeply sloped site. The layered frame emerges from the hillside and breaks free of its skin with a mid-level mass that harbors the entry. A shallow-pitched roof satisfies the required height envelope, while a curved soffit hovers above a centerpiece crescent window that terminates a central spine of the upper level. The rhythm created by rows of floor-to-ceiling windows organizes the elevation and confers generous views to the upper-level living spaces. Weather-resistant ivory-hued stucco replaces classic clapboard siding on the Hampton-like façade, set off by rustic stone and a horizontal band that breaks the vertical

scale of the house. Carved deep into the hillside, a retaining wall borders the north and east sides of the lower level, which harbors the gym, four-car garage and utilities. Walkways and outdoors spaces overlook an indigenous landscape that steps toward the gently rolling foothills that eventually confront the sea. A curved stair and rail lead up from the streetscape to the mid-level entry, which eases the transition from ground level to the main gallery. The foyer and forward stairs add vertical volume to the front of the plan—and lend dignity to a wide-open interior focused on inner-space vistas and outdoor views. Simple, massive forms and coffered ceilings define an innovative plan that invites the exploration of its splendid architectural geometry. Sited toward the ocean, the forward formal rooms take in magnifi-

Crowned by cove lighting and a sculpted ceiling, the living room captures considerable volume under the shallow roof pitch. A centerpiece crescent window establishes a visual link to the outdoors, allows sunlight and reveals glimpses of scenery, even when the drapes are closed.

Left: Richly patterned ceilings in the family room and throughout the house received the same careful design attention as the floor plan. Ivory walls and cabinetry frame views of the horizon and plush earth-toned furnishings. An elegantly crafted mantle harbors a fireplace with a granite surround.

Opposite page: Skylights brighten the upper-level gallery, which defines the formal zone and provides a transition to the casual living area. The unexpected introduction of natural light creates a friendly entry sequence that improves the whole-house function and establishes an informal ambience.

Left: Comfortable stairs draw guests up from the entry to the living-level gallery, where an openness between spaces invites the eye to roam the architectural geometry. Crown molding finished with flat enamel flatters Brazilian cherry floors and stirs the formal environment with a contemporary look.

Right: A barrel-vaulted ceiling adds vertical volume in the gourmet kitchen, which adjoins a spacious nook. Two skylights increase natural light in this north-facing area, enriching the dark Italian cherry cabinets and smooth granite countertops. A hub of family activities, the space converts to a servery for planned events held in the formal dining room.

Opposite page: Dramatic interplays of architecture and rich furnishings express the owners' love of art, books and Eastern décor. Built-in bookshelves border ocean views and display souvenirs of the owners' travels. Thick cornices repeat the horizontal banding that wraps around the exterior of the house.

Right: Designed to embrace a graceful round table that seats eight, the formal dining room provides rows of windows that wrap the space with powerful outdoor views. A dome conceals lighting that accentuates the circular theme—inspired by travels to the Far East. Woven shades minimize glare from the southern California sun.

Left: The owners' retreat boasts separate lavs, a rambling walk-in closet designed for two, an oversized shower and a step-up whirlpool tub. Linen storage tucked beneath the marble-topped vanities streamlines the smooth contours of the space. A curved piece of glass opens the master bath to a spectacular coastal vista.

Opposite page: The architectural character of the home permits the master suite to project beyond the perimeter of the side elevation. A massive column acts as a pedestal to the cylindrical bay—a highly sculpted form capped by wide overhangs. The high-glam spa reiterates the curvature and takes in views that soothe the soul.

Right: In the lower-level game room, comfortable armchair seating surrounds a tech-savvy media system that includes a 50-inch television screen and discreet whole-house speakers. The ceiling pattern and colors serve to separate the play and entertainment spaces. Sliding glass doors connect the area to a covered patio and terrace.

cent sunsets and allow plenty of daylight through the south wall of windows. Ideas brewed for the future must also satisfy the essential daily functions of a practical home. The well-equipped kitchen serves as a hub for many activities and features a spacious nook that encourages impromptu family gatherings. Italian cherry cabinets frame stainless-steel appliances, granite countertops and a variety of contemporary accessories, such as steel brackets and hanging rods. A privacy door links the hardworking servery area of the kitchen with the formal dining room—an arrangement that invites planned events. The lower level of the home includes a gym, two home offices, an additional bedroom and a game room.

Left: Like the portholes of a yacht, round windows line the waterside of the elevation, allowing glimpses of the sea. The second level harbors sleeping quarters and a rear deck—cantilevered above the garage and deliberately tucked in from the street.

Right: A whimsical curved dormer cradles the upper-level master bath in a captured space that is both futuristic and serene. Exposed structural elements and a cool color palette evoke the charm of the early freely crafted cottages of the Northeastern seaboard.

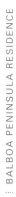

Cottage charm gives way to an urbane new-century character in the master bedroom, where sculpted pieces evocative of a ship's bow frame spectacular waterfront views. Varying ceiling lines convey a delightful informality that's keyed to the character of the site.

intimate themes to resolve its ample spaces and large scale. A wide-open arrangement of the public rooms allows definitive areas—the kitchen, living and dining rooms—to overlap. Articulated by an eclectic array of forms, such as a freestanding aquarium and a *banco*-style low wall, the interior achieves a sense of unity with serene textures and sensual furnishings. On the third floor, the owners' retreat boldly rambles from a prominent forward deck to a private rear portico. A palette of sculpted forms plays counterpoint to a relaxed new-century character in the bedroom, where great views mingle with vintage décor. Designed to convey the sense of a quaint, renovated attic space, the master suite confronts spectacular scenery with symbols of the adventurous architecture of early American cottages: varied ceiling lines, exposed structural elements and curved dormer windows.

Sandover | RESIDENCE ONE

LOCATION: HUNTINGTON BEACH, CALIFORNIA
BUILDER: HEARTHSIDE HOMES

PHOTOGRAPHY: JEFFREY ARON 2001

3,457 SQUARE FEET

Near the entry, French doors lead to a den that flexes to a home office. The drive penetrates the side of the plan, framed by a detached optional space that inspires the imagination and contributes a full sense of entry to the home.

Sandover | Biking distance from the coolest strip of sand in California—Huntington Beach, the original Surf City USA—a new community of sixteen houses boasts walkable streets, ocean views and leading-edge architecture. Not far from Bolsa Chica State Park, the neighborhood honors its proximity to the coastal preserve with seamless integrations of indoors and out. Courtyards and porte cocheres influence the street scene, enriching shingle-clad or stucco façades. Openings in the perimeter of this traditional elevation mingle the benefits of the fresh sea air and plenty of daylight with magnificent views captured to the front and rear of the plan. A smart arrangement of formal and casual spaces surrounds a lose-the-shoes courtyard and a massive outdoor fireplace.

Well lit and airy, the gourmet kitchen provides space for easy meals as well as a serve-yourself tea and coffee area. New-century appliances and vintage cabinetry surround an ample preparation counter ready-made for planned events.

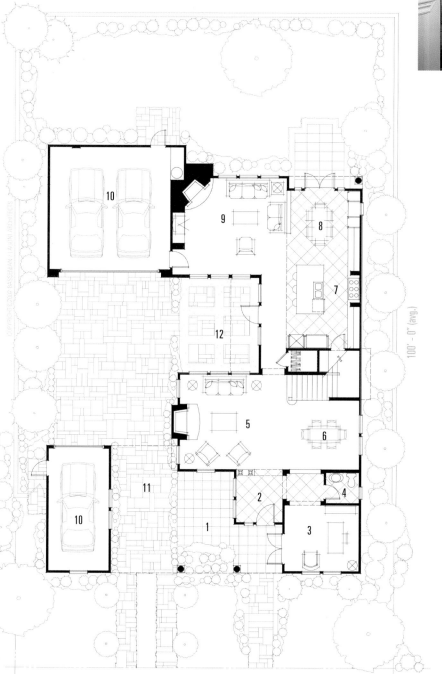

60' - 0" (avg.)   **First Floor**

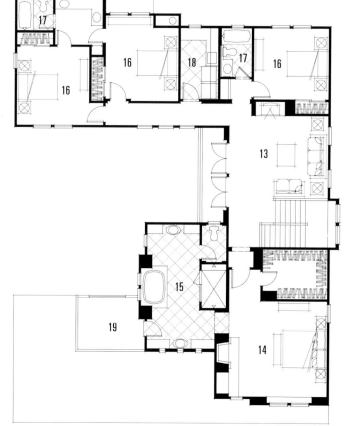

Second Floor

1 Porch	6 Dining Room	11 Porte Cochere	16 Bedroom
2 Entry	7 Kitchen	12 Courtyard	17 Bathroom
3 Den/Office	8 Nook	13 Teen Area	18 Laundry
4 Powder Room	9 Family Room	14 Master Suite	19 Deck
5 Living Room	10 Garage	15 Master Bath	

Shoreline at The Boardwalk : RESIDENCE ONE

LOCATION: HUNTINGTON BEACH, CALIFORNIA
BUILDER: CHRISTOPHER HOMES

PHOTOGRAPHY: JOHN R. BARE 2002

3.388 SQUARE FEET

A catalog of architectural styles defines this California coastal cottage—a rich mix of bungalow, traditional and seaside elements. In a neighborhood of compact lots, this C-shaped design creates open spatial relationships inside the plan and great links to the outdoors all the way around.

Shoreline at The Boardwalk : Stone, lap siding and cedar shingles set off this sand-colored coastal cottage, creating the profound appeal of an established seaside elevation. The house's California bungalow-inspired character, evocative of an early Craftsman vernacular, shows in the side-gabled façade, tapered columns, high-gloss white trim and double-hung windows. Nostalgic elements—truncated stone pillars and a simple balustrade—line an inviting front porch that recalls the American cottages of gentler times. In keeping with the pedestrian-friendly nature of the *Boardwalk* community, the thoughtful, compact layout is equipped with a rear garage, allowing the drive to double as a multiple-use courtyard. A

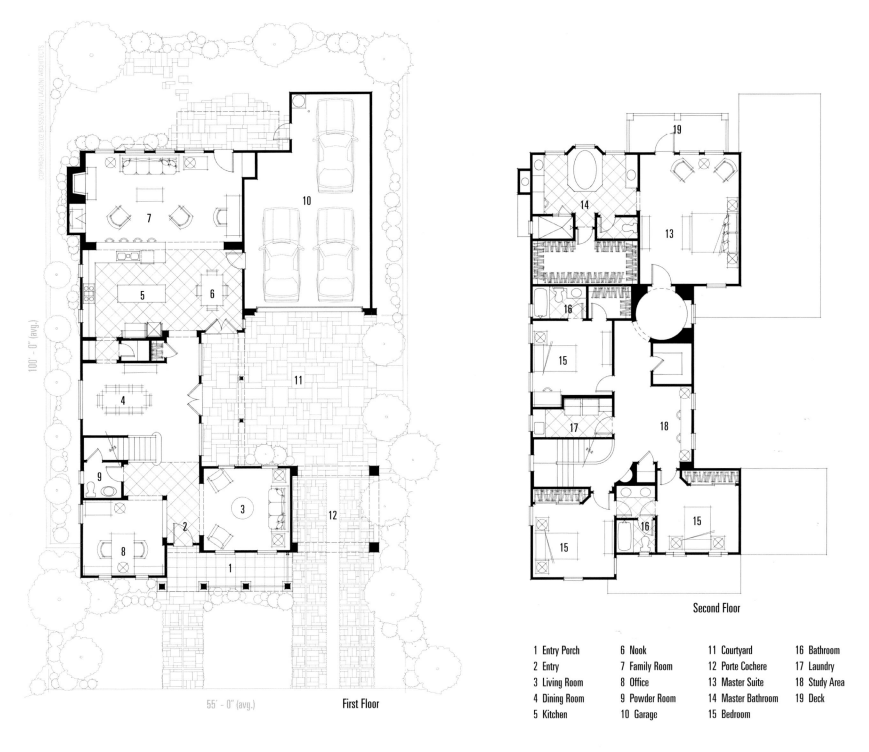

First Floor

55' - 0" (avg.)

100' - 0" (avg.)

Second Floor

1 Entry Porch	6 Nook	11 Courtyard	16 Bathroom
2 Entry	7 Family Room	12 Porte Cochere	17 Laundry
3 Living Room	8 Office	13 Master Suite	18 Study Area
4 Dining Room	9 Powder Room	14 Master Bathroom	19 Deck
5 Kitchen	10 Garage	15 Bedroom	

graceful porte cochere provides the plan with a detailed extension of its slender footprint and maintains a sense of privacy for the central courtyard. The home integrates a pleasing color palette with a flexible interior that effectively merges high tech with the coastal region's relaxed lifestyles. An easy-flowing floor plan is accomplished by volume spaces and gently rounded arches defining the transitions between well-appointed rooms. The tiled foyer opens to the forward living room and to a den and powder room—a convenient arrangement for a home office. A generous front porch extends the formal living room, linking the inner space with views and a palatable sense of the outdoors. A winding stair with

Berber carpeting weds a tapestry of textures, wall coverings and cornices in the living room—a forward space that is defined by a graceful arch and visually linked to the outdoors toward the front porch and the side courtyard.

hand-finished maple handrails highlights the gallery hall. French doors dress the formal dining room with a casual spirit, inviting guests to linger on the side terrace or explore the night sky from the courtyard. An expansive gourmet kitchen mixes antique-white raised-panel cabinetry and wood floors with state-of-the-art commercial-style appliances and recessed lighting. French doors and tall windows expand the morning nook and family space—carefully placed to the rear of the plan, which leads to a terrace and landscaped yard.

Below: A wood-burning fireplace lends an inviting ambience to the informal living space—carefully placed to the rear of the plan. Fully wired, the home provides high-end media capabilities in the family room.

Above: Raised-panel cabinetry in antique white surrounds stainless-steel appliances in the gourmet kitchen, including a commercial-style six-burner cooktop range and a 42-inch side-by-side refrigerator. A peninsula counter and snack bar extend the food-preparation island.

Right: Separate lavatories set in Pullman cabinets frame a luxury spa-style tub in the master bath. An oversized shower and a detailed vanity border the entry to the walk-in closet, which is designed for two owners.

Opposite page: Carefully planned aesthetics in the master suite contribute to an honest vocabulary of modern influences—both rich and restrained. An impressive rotunda serves as a vestibule connecting the upper gallery hall to the master bedroom. A convenient deck opens the décor to ocean breezes.

Below: An impressive open stair defines the entry space between the formal dining room and the forward den. Wide windows expand the dining area beyond the room's boundaries and grant daylight or night views to planned events.

Shoreline at The Boardwalk | RESIDENCE TWO

LOCATION: HUNTINGTON BEACH, CALIFORNIA
BUILDER: CHRISTOPHER HOMES

PHOTOGRAPHY: JOHN R. BARE 2002

3,722 SQUARE FEET

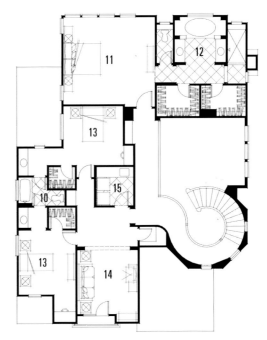

Second Floor

Above: Vintage details inspired by the Northeastern seaboard gently flavor this California coastal cottage. Asymmetrical rooflines set off a charming octagonal turret that allows plenty of natural light within—where a rotunda foyer creates an impressive entry.

Shoreline at The Boardwalk ┊ Pure form meets 21st-century function in this coastal home, which the designer envisioned as a traditional cottage with a California state of mind. Like a romantic seaboard pied-a-terre, the siding-and-stone elevation offers an inviting reminder of gentler times—yet steps into the future with an unbalanced symmetry and a smart use of space. Located within the gated community of *The Boardwalk* at Huntington Beach, the four-bedroom home is only a few hundred yards from the Pacific—securely rooted in its own neighborhood yet an easy walk to the beach. Honey-toned maple hardwood floors unify the formal spaces, which frame the entry rotunda and foyer. A winding staircase and maple rail highlight the open arrangement of rooms, granting volume and a sense of high style to a relaxed ambience. A row of clerestory windows enhances a triple-window view in the formal dining room, providing a strong connection to the outdoors and bringing in plenty of natural light. The strength of the plan lies in its simplicity, providing an axial relationship between the public and

Opposite page: A row of recessed clerestory windows suggesting a nautical theme overlooks an open arrangement of the formal rooms. Columns help to define the space, which offers grand views through a wall of glass in the formal dining room.

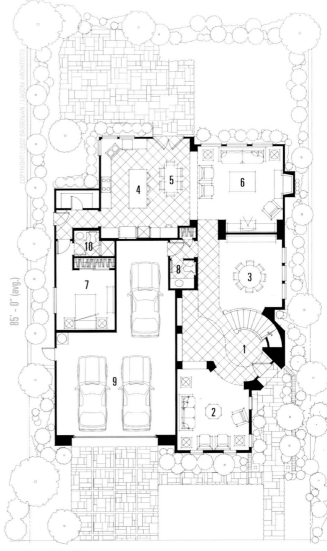

1 Entry
2 Living Room
3 Dining Room
4 Kitchen
5 Nook
6 Family Room
7 Guest Room
8 Powder Room
9 Garage
10 Bathroom
11 Master Suite
12 Master Bathroom
13 Bedroom
14 Teen Room
15 Laundry

First Floor   46' - 0" (avg.)

European-style cabinetry and cutting-edge culinary appliances mix it up in the gourmet kitchen—a well-organized space that opens to a spacious morning nook and to the multi-purpose courtyard through French doors.

private realms. A barrel-arched hallway opens the front of the plan to the casual living area—an inviting space designed for great views and excellent outdoor flow. A subdued palette of earth tones embraces traditional elements, such as a focal-point fireplace with a white-enameled mantel and surround. Provincial elements mix it up with the clean lines of cutting-edge appliances in the well-organized kitchen, which provides generous counters and food-preparation space for two cooks. An ample walk-through pantry with a service door leads to an expansive suite designed to accommodate a guest or live-in relative. French doors lead from the morning nook to a covered entertainment patio.

A coffered ceiling with boxed wood beams highlights the living room, enhanced by views through tall windows. Hardwood floors, muted hues and comfortable decorative cushions add a twist of put-your-feet-up attitude to this refined formal space.

Secluded to the rear of the upper-level plan, the master suite provides great views through a wall of tall windows. An upholstered settee in butternut gets along just fine with an earthy palette of sunshine walls, maple floors and a sienna-hued sisal rug.

Clifton Heights | RESIDENCE TWO

LOCATION: LADERA RANCH, CALIFORNIA
BUILDER: CENTEX HOMES, SOUTH COAST DIVISION

PHOTOGRAPHY: ERIC FIGGE 2002

3,597 SQUARE FEET

A porte cochere links an optional single-car garage with the main house and lends privacy to the courtyard behind them. The structure offers a short, sheltered commute when the detached space converts to a home office.

Clifton Heights | Set among the rugged hills of Ladera Ranch not far from the Southern California coast, this traditional home takes on the rhythm of an expanded seaside cottage, with a wide elevation clad in white clapboard siding. In a community rich with diverse architecture—from Spanish Colonial to Cape Cod—the design works against convention with clean lines and a cool, uncluttered façade. A trio of dormers lends a degree of formality that contradicts the playfulness of graceful arches and a sculpted porte cochere. Stone pillars and rugged accents ground the structure with careful detail and convey a sense of the past. Intimating early Southern houses, the cross-gabled roofline expresses a single-story design—a deliberate strategy that provides layering and further defines the two-story ele-

White clapboard siding and wide windows on the rear elevation convey a sense of informality and create an inviting atmosphere for entertaining. The sunroom offers natural light to the interior and eases the transition from the casual living area to the outdoors.

1 Entry Porch	8 Guest Room	15 Porte Cochere
2 Entry	9 Bathroom	16 Butler's Pantry
3 Living Room	10 Sun Room	17 Master Suite
4 Dining Room	11 Powder Room	18 Master Bathroom
5 Kitchen	12 Office/Garage	19 Bedroom
6 Nook	13 Garage	20 Laundry
7 Family Room	14 Courtyard	21 Deck

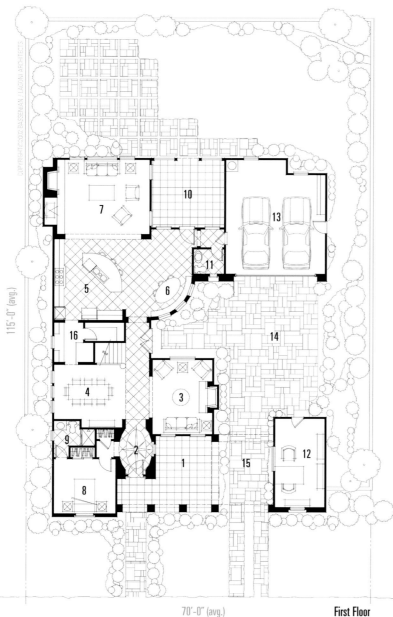

115'-0" (avg.)

70'-0" (avg.)

First Floor

Second Floor

Southern Hills | RESIDENCE TWO

LOCATION: COTO DE CAZA, CALIFORNIA
BUILDER: LENNAR HOMES

PHOTOGRAPHY: JOHN R. BARE 1998

4,102 SQUARE FEET

Low-pitched rooflines integrated with a hipped form define the layered elevation. A Dutch gable helps to break the close massing yet achieves a sense of unity with vertical windows and clapboard siding keyed to the exterior. Masonry pillars and a graceful arch at the entry establish a pleasing rhythm against the cool backdrop of traditional California colors.

Southern Hills | Surrounded by rolling hills on the cusp of the Saddleback Mountains, the golf and tennis community at Coto de Caza boasts diverse translations of Mediterranean and traditional vernaculars. In a neighborhood of spacious inland lots, this 4,000-square-foot coastal design evokes the charm of a breezy seaside cottage, with clean lines and classic horizontal siding. A sense of informality softens traditional lines and brings a new look to the eco-sensitive streetscape. The façade further responds to the spirit of the neighborhood by turning the forward garage to the side, with the single-car garage set back from the side-walk. White enamel balustrades, headers and window trim play counterpoint to a sand-hued

Generous windows sited toward the spectacular fairway open the rear elevation to the scenery and a sense of nature. Triple windows and French doors blur the lines between inside and out, and allow breezes and daylight to fill the open interior. A balcony extends the master suite, protected by a trellis that controls the light into the owners' bedroom and retreat.

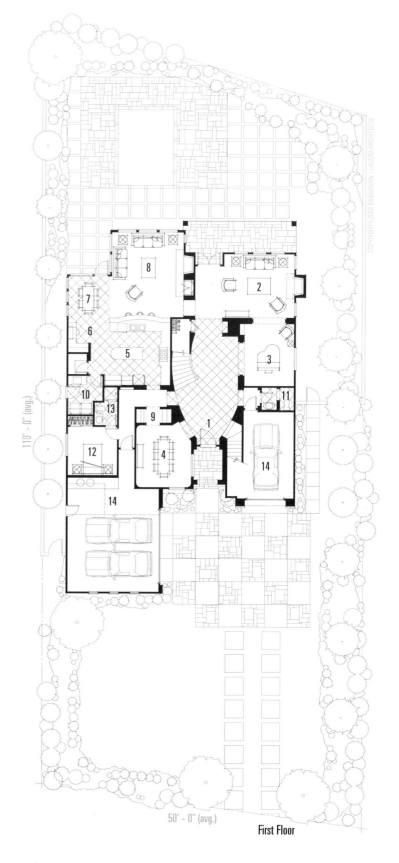

110' - 0" (avg.)

50' - 0" (avg.)

First Floor

Second Floor

1 Entry	11 Powder Room
2 Living Room	12 Bedroom
3 Den/Music Room	13 Bathroom
4 Dining Room	14 Garage
5 Kitchen	15 Master Suite
6 Family Organize Center	16 Master Retreat
7 Nook	17 Master Bathroom
8 Family Room	18 Guest Bedroom, Home Office
9 Butler's Pantry	19 Study Area
10 Laundry	

Left: The gourmet kitchen and nook grant ample space for the home's organizing center—a convenient command central that extends the casual area and allows space for computers and calendars. A marble countertop provides an overlook to the family room and a place for on-the-go meals and family conversations.

Right: A cool palette embraces plush furnishings, built-in cabinetry and a baby grand piano in the music room—a secondary public space that extends the formal living zone. Square arches define the area and softly echo the neo-Victorian theme established by the central gallery.

elevation and brick pedestals along the drive. A magnificent two-story entry hall draws on the Victorian origins of the plan form, allowing the central gallery to function as a hub of circulation and organizing center. The house conceals its intentions from the open foyer yet seamlessly links the public and private realms, and provides views that extend to the rear of the plan. Clerestory windows bring natural light to the core of the home and announce a secondary formal space that is adjacent to the living room: a comfortable music room or den that harbors built-ins and allows daylight from the side yard. Uniquely placed to capture spectacular golf course views, the living room breaks the forward-formal zone pattern and offers a delightful ambience that invites planned events. The central gallery defines the boundaries of the informal realm, framed by walls of glass that bring in a sense of the great outdoors.

A gently curved stair rail enhances the entry space and breaks the rigidity imposed by vertical proportions and high volume. The contemporary use of space mixes fluidly with the Victorian central gallery—juxtaposing traditional elements with futuristic dimensions and recessed lighting. A massive square arch that leads to the music room reaches toward a triplet of clerestory windows.

Chapter Four

SMALL-LOT DETACHED HOMES

Conventional California lots used to "live" in the neighborhood of 6,000 square feet—less than a decade ago, that figure dropped to 5,000. These days, a property must shrink to around 4,500 square feet for the market to call it small. The past decade's *de rigueur* portfolio of plans fit for a lot 35- to 50-feet wide is too easy, and there are plenty of patio and zero-lot-line houses to prove it. Recently, Bassenian/Lagoni Architects took on a bigger challenge and started a wave in the West, creating livable, hardworking environments with soaring spaces, satisfying views and individual outdoor places—for very narrow, high-density home sites. BLA championed 2-Pac™ and Pocket Lot™ designs, which allow adjoining properties to press snugly against one another yet maintain the owners' privacy. The ground rules are few: create viable, spacious environments with whole-house appeal, choose wonderful communities in which to build and *always* keep it exciting.

Lighthouse at The Boardwalk : RESIDENCE ONE

LOCATION: HUNTINGTON BEACH, CALIFORNIA
BUILDER: CHRISTOPHER HOMES

PHOTOGRAPHY: JOHN R. BARE 2002

2,456 SQUARE FEET

A porte cochere separates the rear-positioned garage from the street scene, permitting the drive to extend the dimensions of the central courtyard. Deeply recessed windows and a sheltered entry convey European traditions and lend a sense of dignity to the façade.

Lighthouse at The Boardwalk ⋮ Smooth stucco walls, wrought-iron details and a well-placed courtyard inspired by the architecture of southern Spain take on a new look in one of three signature homes in this California coastal community. A neighborhood of eclectic exterior styles, *The Boardwalk* at Huntington Beach juxtaposes historic vernaculars with crisp modern elements, creating an architectural dialect that is both cutting-edge and comfortable. Sited toward the central courtyard, the plan captures a wealth of daylight and permits an easy transition to the outside from formal and casual spaces. Richly varied architectural elements, such as a massive indoor fireplace and an arcaded porch, contribute to the luxurious impression of the home. A restrained décor reveals a fidelity to the Spanish Colonial vernacular that is enhanced by a fluid relationship with the outdoors. A recessed paneled door, nested in a sculpted entryway, opens to the foyer and living room—rich with natural light and a relaxed California ambience. Elegant hand-finished maple balustrades depict a Moorish influence—a quatrefoil pattern that contradicts space-age curves, sleek accents and subtle recessed lighting. The architectural style is further defined by tall muntin windows, arches and radial walls that establish a rural European connection.

Wrought-iron balustrades add definition to an arcade protecting the upper loggia—an outdoor space that extends the boundaries of the master suite. A radial wall is the outer expression of a rotunda vestibule on the upper level.

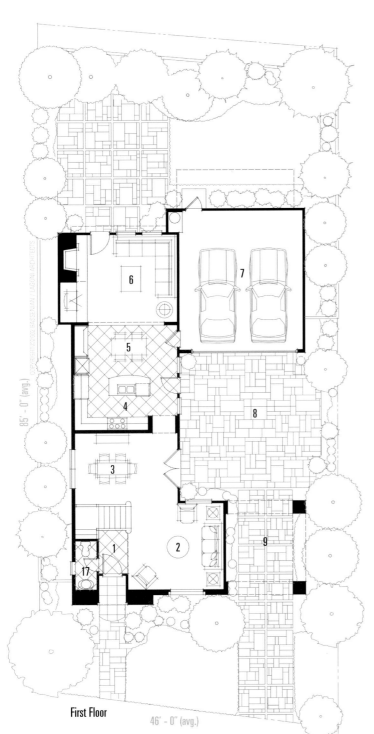

First Floor

46' - 0" (avg.)

1 Entry

2 Living Room

3 Dining Room

4 Kitchen

5 Nook

6 Family Room

7 Garage

8 Courtyard

9 Porte Cochere

10 Den

11 Laundry

12 Bedroom

13 Bathroom

14 Master Suite

15 Master Bathroom

16 Deck

17 Powder Room

Second Floor

Below: Tall windows on two sides of the parlor-sized living room bring in daylight and views from both the front and central courtyards. Rich tones of sienna and cedar enhance a formal space designed for short periods of entertaining.

Above: Plenty of amenities highlight the gourmet kitchen, linked to the formal dining room by an arched passageway. A serene palette and bold perspectives nudge Euro elements to a new edge without losing their retro cool.

A careful sequence of rooms permits the plan to proceed organically from the formal zones, framing the entry to a casual living area that is sited toward the rear terrace and property. Views extend the living room out to a versatile courtyard, where a profusion of plants adds a sense of intimacy. An archway connects the formal dining room to the food-preparation and serving area of the gourmet kitchen. A French door and two tall windows bring in plenty of natural light, while an open arrangement of rooms allows the kitchen and nook stunning interior vistas and outdoor views through the family room. On the upper floor, a gallery hall overlooking the courtyard links two secondary bedrooms and a den. The loft or landing area allows space for computers, books and games, and provides additional storage. Two outdoor decks flank a generous master bedroom—one is oriented toward the rear property, while a decorative deck or upper loggia provides an intimate view of the center courtyard.

Opposite page: Rich with historic character, the entry foyer opens directly to the formal rooms, where glass walls and French doors invite fresh air and daylight to mingle with sensually comfortable rooms.

Lighthouse at The Boardwalk : RESIDENCE TWO

LOCATION: HUNTINGTON BEACH, CALIFORNIA
BUILDER: CHRISTOPHER HOMES

PHOTOGRAPHY: JOHN R. BARE 2002

2,654 SQUARE FEET

Classic elements set off an engaging blend of vernacular styles on this rustic façade—concealing a thoroughly contemporary interior that is fully wired for the future. Traditional transoms, moldings and grilles deck out the elevation, juxtaposed with broadband capabilities and a computer hub indoors.

Lighthouse at The Boardwalk : Firmly rooted in the native vernacular of the West, this two-story coastal cottage is positioned on a 4,800-square-foot lot in the highly desirable *Boardwalk* neighborhood of Huntington Beach. Part of a limited edition of sixty-five residences sequestered behind a gated entrance a few hundred yards from the beach, the house's simple, honest forms and vintage seaboard details convey a poetic symmetry. A single-story fascia above the garage adjusts the façade to pleasing, human-scale proportions. Influenced by time-honored revival architecture, the elevation blends elements of the Shingle style complemented by colonial detailing.

Maple hardwood floors unify an eclectic nouveau décor—rich with weaves and faux-exotic fabrics. Pure architectural elements define the separation between the formal rooms, allowing daylight to penetrate the interior.

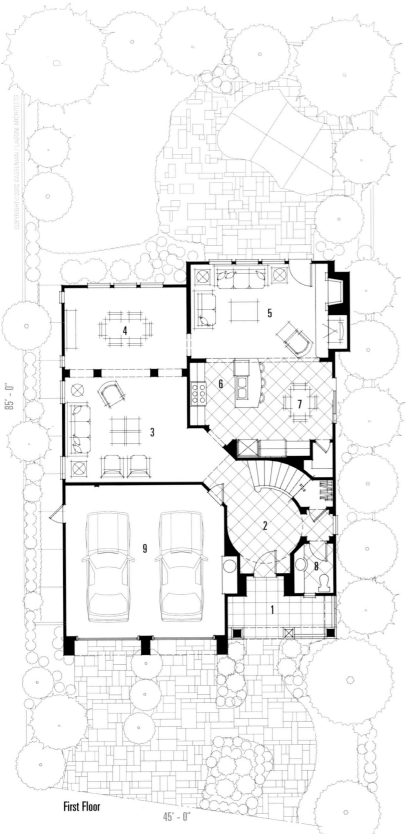

First Floor

45' - 0"

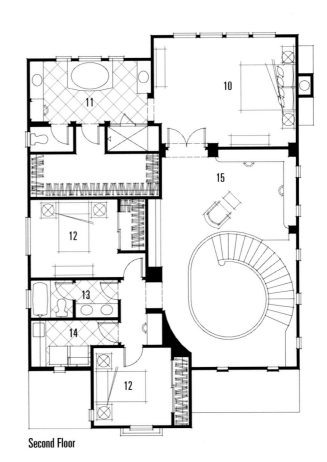

Second Floor

1 Entry Porch	6 Kitchen	11 Master Bathroom
2 Entry	7 Nook	12 Bedroom
3 Living Room	8 Powder Room	13 Bathroom
4 Dining Room	9 Garage	14 Laundry
5 Family Room	10 Master Suite	15 Loft

Right: An upper-level loft provides ample space for computers and books—and easily converts to a den or library. Banana-hued walls embrace a symmetrical arrangement of space that provides an into-the-future look for this flex area.

Left: A winding staircase intimates the quiet curves of the arches and angled walls of the distinctive interior, which unfolds gradually from the two-story foyer. A white balustrade and maple railing frame the computer loft.

Bold, white columns and stone pillars frame the front porch against a backdrop of rich chocolate shingle siding, complemented by classic white trim. A signature color palette that includes sienna and cedar enhances period details and a box-paneled entry. Prevailing summer breezes find their way through a straightforward interior that boasts carefully defined formal and casual spaces. Arched passages, triple windows and French doors allow natural light to flow easily through the main-level rooms. A circular two-story foyer surrounds a softly winding staircase that leads to an upper-level loft designed to easily convert to command central for the home's computer systems. Downstairs, an angled gallery hall opens to the formal rooms, which relate to the casual living space and gourmet kitchen through flattened arches.

Massive shapes surround the formal dining room, where a bold color palette enlivens the room's character. Form and function create harmony around a wide wall of glass granting daylight or moonlight.

New-century stainless-steel amenities and a well-organized serving area in the gourmet kitchen invite planned events. A food preparation island equipped with a vegetable sink overlooks the morning nook—a convenient place for casual meals.

Arden Square | RESIDENCES ONE & TWO

LOCATION: IRVINE, CALIFORNIA
BUILDER: BROOKFIELD HOMES

PHOTOGRAPHY: JEFFREY ARON 2000

RESIDENCE ONE - 1,631 SQUARE FEET
RESIDENCE TWO - 1,776 SQUARE FEET

Arden Square | Designed to coexist with a wide selection of exterior styles, these innovative, award-winning residences create an eclectic partnership in this planned Irvine community—harbored within the established neighborhood of Northwood. The adjoining compact lots share a staggered zipperline boundary that allows the properties to press snugly against one another. In order to maximize land use and maintain privacy for both homeowners, the 2-Pac™ configuration is a Bassenian/Lagoni innovation that pairs a home with a forward garage (Residence Two) next to a house planned with the garage to the rear (Residence One). The recessed garage permits a forecourt—an outside space that offers an area for play as well as an outdoor view enjoyed by the formal dining room. Residence One also employs a bay window to bring daylight into the kitchen and morning nook. Residence Two provides well-defined public and private zones, with the tiled entry opening to a formal space with a winding stair. Upper-level sleeping quarters include a spacious owners' suite and two secondary bedrooms that share a hall leading to a full bath and laundry.

Opposite page above: Residence One features a forward kitchen and nook, enhanced by a bay window—which provides a visual link to the neighborhood. Plenty of cabinets and counter space surround a portable food preparation island, facilitating casual meals as well as planned events.

Opposite page below: Residence Two provides an expansive informal living space that unites a gourmet kitchen and traditional dining area. A contemporary island counter complements the provincial cabinetry of the L-shaped kitchen and overlooks a stunning family room that brings in views and light.

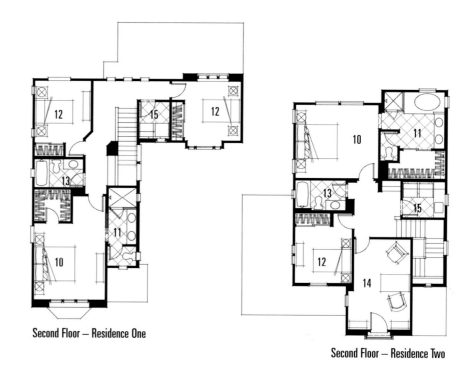

Second Floor — Residence One

Second Floor — Residence Two

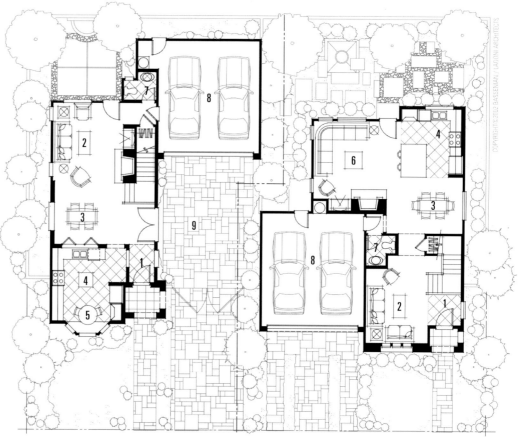

First Floor — Residence One

First Floor — Residence Two

1 Entry	6 Family Room	11 Master Bathroom
2 Living Room	7 Powder Room	12 Bedroom
3 Dining Room	8 Garage	13 Bathroom
4 Kitchen	9 Courtyard/Drive	14 Bedroom/Study/Office
5 Nook	10 Master Suite	15 Laundry

Chapter Five

ON-THE-BOARD PROJECTS

Geographically diverse, the portfolio of projects on the drawing boards at Bassenian/Lagoni Architects conveys a movable flavor, a clean dynamic that is utterly prepared for change. Less formal than their 20th-century predecessors, the new designs take on the future with a smarter use of space, replacing a frenzy of amenities with flexible, well-planned rooms. Cities now desire smaller houses on fewer lots, while homebuyers want where they live to do more in a wide-open, wind-in-the-hair environment. BLA's position in resolving the divergence is to satisfy today's highly sophisticated market with a tomorrow home that is different by design. The smart sample of projects-in-progress in this section demonstrates how hard-working and neighborhood-friendly houses can be. Fresh and evolved, the homes approach their singular heritage honestly—with diverse styles and interiors so intelligent they can afford to be simple yet breathtakingly stunning.

Shady Canyon Custom Residence

LOCATION: IRVINE, CALIFORNIA
BUILDER: WARMINGTON HOMES

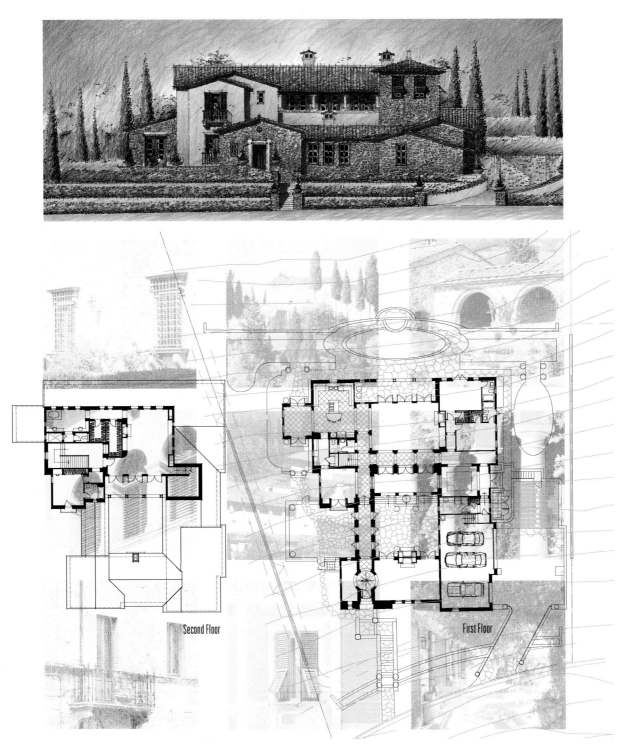

Second Floor

First Floor

Shady Canyon Custom Residence | Clay-tile roofs crown this rustic stone-and-stucco façade, enhanced by wood surrounds, shutters and simple forms. The custom plan's proposed forward orientation will permit a sloped site in Shady Canyon, inviting views from four sides. A rich palette evocative of a Tuscan farmhouse enhances the layered and highly textured elevation—a composite of organic, individual forms that appear to have been added over time, expressing a vital habitat.

Benchley Hill at Amerige Heights | RESIDENCE TWO

LOCATION: FULLERTON, CALIFORNIA
BUILDER: PARDEE HOMES

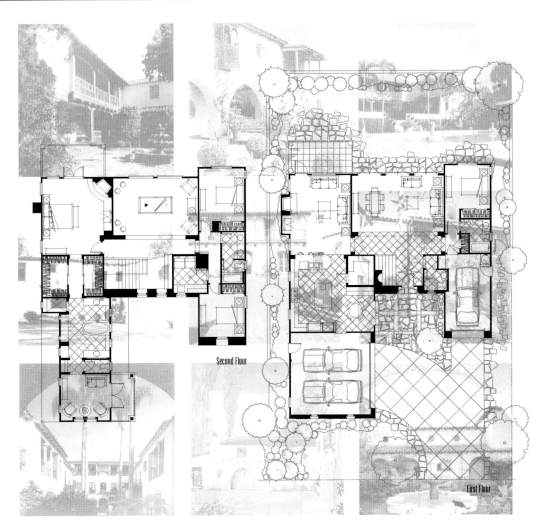

Second Floor

First Floor

Benchley Hill | Slated for the new neighborhood of Benchley Hill at Amerige Heights in the city of Fullerton, this Early California elevation features a split-garage configuration with a swing drive that diminishes garage presence at the streetscape. A detailed wrought- iron gate leads to an intimate entry court that announces a straight- forward interior designed for a disciplined footprint. Natural light advances the playful spirit of the home, with plenty of outdoor spaces and a forward Monterey-style balcony.

The Ranch at Santa Monica | RESIDENCES TWO & FOUR

LOCATION: RANCHO SANTA FE, CALIFORNIA
BUILDER: WESTERN PACIFIC HOMES

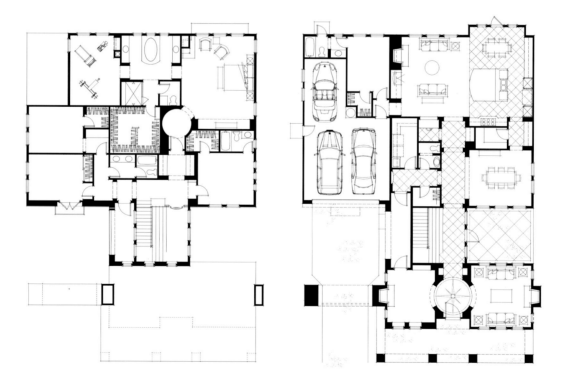

Residence Two | Surrounded by San Diego's most prestigious locales—Fairbanks Ranch, Santa Luz, Rancho Santa Fe and Del Mar—*The Ranch at Santa Monica* breaks ground where legends tread. High-glam ranchos created for moguls and stars by well-

known 20th-century designers such as Wallace Neff and Lilian Rice populate the region. The elite enclave of seventy-two future houses will honor the historic surroundings with artful Hispanic architecture that is at home with its Hollywood-era neighbors.

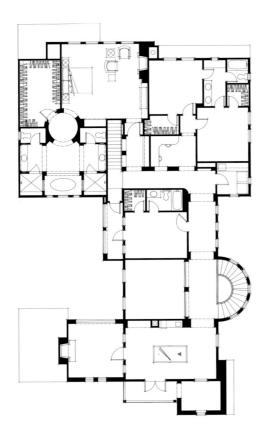
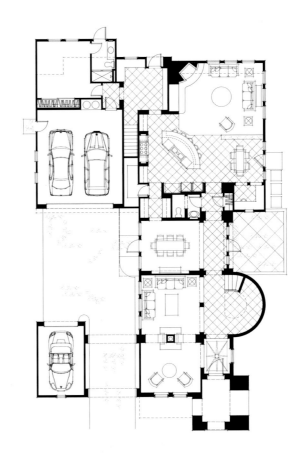

Residence Four | Sweeping views of serene, rolling terrain will surround this 21st-century adaptation of Early California design—a refined plan that stays true to its colonial origins. A wrought-iron gate that hides the motor court reinforces the style and offsets a Monterey-style balcony and a battered wall that frame the entry. Inside, a spectacular circular staircase and an open, two-story living room subdue a high-volume entry. A rear staircase increases circulation while improving function for the family's living space.

Renaissance | RESIDENCES ONE & TWO

LOCATION: NOVATO, CALIFORNIA
BUILDER: DAVIDON HOMES

DIGITAL IMAGERY: FOCUS 360 ARCHITECTURAL COMMUNICATIONS

First Floor

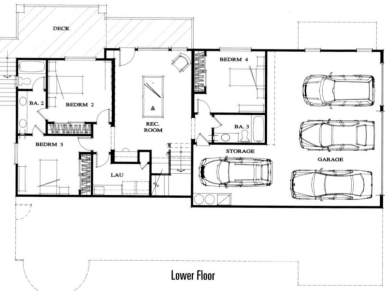

Lower Floor

Residence One | Slated for the rolling hills west of Novato—a mere twenty-nine miles north of San Francisco—this golf-course community will feature an eclectic menu of styles. Indigenous growth and preserved trees will reinforce, rather than defy, the site's organized response to the lay of the land. Individual semi-custom plans will sprawl across wooded lots designed to take full advantage of fairway views. A central formal zone permits plenty of natural light to enter the home.

Residence Two | A solid tile roof sets off an impressive ensemble of forms with this virtual elevation—which plays Early California and Tuscan influences against the serene character of a resort home. Two forward gables harbor the garages and employ a forward turret to contain an arrangement of tall windows and concomitant dual porticos, which further break the massing. The entire rear perimeter of the five-bedroom plan opens to views of the golf course and undulating hills beyond.

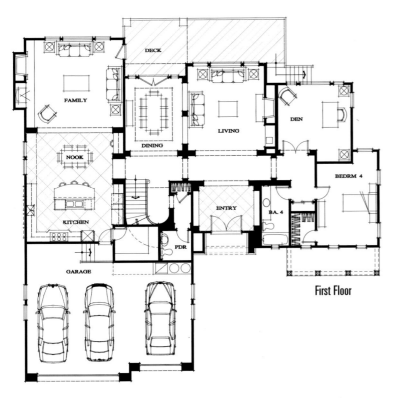

First Floor

Second Floor

Shady Canyon | RESIDENCES ONE & TWO

LOCATION: IRVINE, CALIFORNIA
BUILDER: GREYSTONE HOMES

Shady Canyon will preserve its indigenous grasses, rock outcroppings and coastal sage scrub to synchronize its landscape to the rugged beauty of the San Joaquin Hills. An architectural palette influenced by early Tuscan and Andalusian styles is designed to suit the informal, highly secluded locale.

Residence One | A simple gated entry introduces this Early California plan at Shady Canyon—a golf course community that is already on good terms with the environment. Less than a mile from Irvine's arterial freeway, the development's 1,070 acres of pristine real estate will allow new home-buyers room to breathe, surrounded by an incremental 800 wild acres protected as public land. The plan's narrow breezeway opens to a forecourt that proceeds to the formal entry and beyond to a larger central courtyard. The foyer leads immediately to a flexible bedroom/home office and to a main gallery that wraps the courtyard. Casual living space includes a primary kitchen for food preparation as well as a secondary or culinary area for serving.

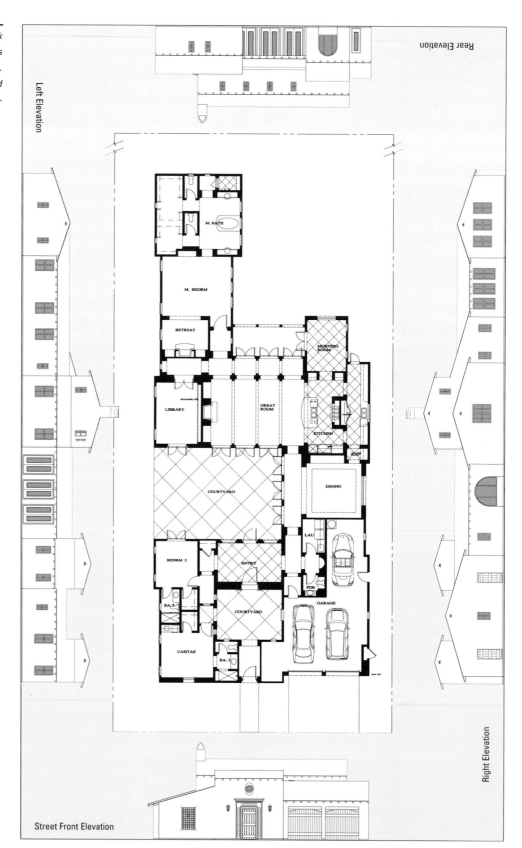

Rear Elevation

Left Elevation

Right Elevation

Street Front Elevation

M. BATH

M. BEDRM

RETREAT

MORNING ROOM

LIBRARY

GREAT ROOM

KITCHEN

COURTYARD

DINING

LAU

BEDRM 2

ENTRY

PDR

GARAGE

BA 3

COURTYARD

CASITAS

BA 3

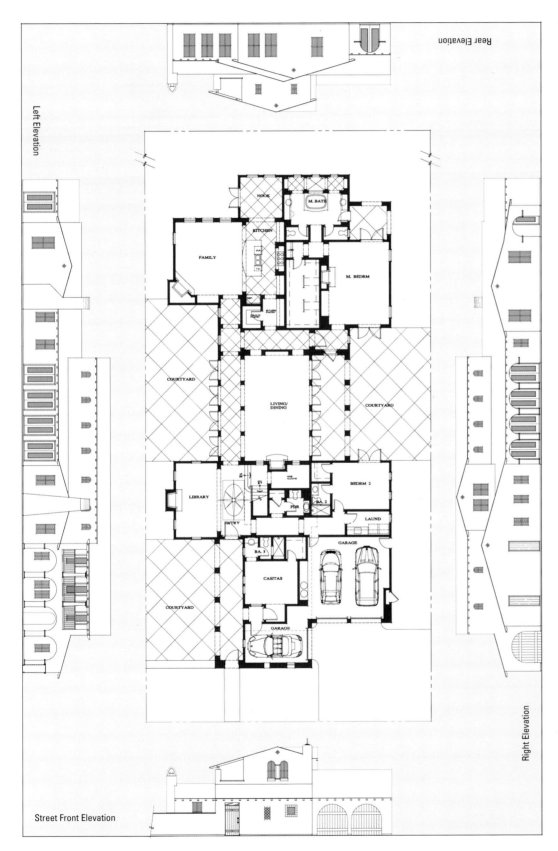

Left Elevation

Rear Elevation

Right Elevation

Street Front Elevation

NOOK

M. BATH

KITCHEN

FAMILY

M. BEDRM

COURTYARD

LIVING/
DINING

COURTYARD

LIBRARY

BEDRM 2

PDR

BA. 2

ENTRY

LAUND

BA. 3

GARAGE

CASITAS

COURTYARD

GARAGE

Rural elements of genuine Hispanic parentage will create an almost primal correspondence between this house and the wild, open space that surrounds it. True to its provenance, the design frames outer space with interior living areas and boldly mixes natural landscapes with well-defined rooms. An upper level provides flex space or additional sleeping quarters.

Residence Two ⋮ Derived from the indigenous architecture of southern Spain, this colonial revival plan organizes a series of side courtyards around the interior. An understated entry gate progresses to an expansive arcade or loggia—a sheltered procession that is interrupted by the open *casita* to the side of the house. The formal entry occurs between the library and the stairs, and announces an axial gallery framed by the formal living/dining room and an open courtyard. Interior vistas and outdoor views reinforce a ceremonial approach to the private realm. The informal zone clusters an open kitchen with a spacious family room that shares the warmth of its fireplace with this area of the home. A rambling master retreat includes a sunlit sitting space and access to the side courtyard.

Afterword
by Carl Lagoni, AIA

Ten years ago Bassenian/Lagoni stopped to search its collective soul. We tore apart our processes. We re-examined the root concepts of our design. What generally had passed for, say, "Mediterranean" in the '70s and '80s—white stucco topped by a red-tile roof—was thoroughly de-constructed. We began to search for a better solution. For us, the home of the future became the house of the past.

As part of our research, we began a long look backward. We explored the evolution of housing in Europe and embraced its long-accumulated layers of tradition. We traveled to various parts of our own country to observe the roots of American residential architecture. What evolved over the last few years, depicted in the preceding pages, is a far more exhilarating, more authentic, and more articulated version of "Mediterranean" and other styles. We found a better definition of Andalusian, Tuscan, and French Country. We began to explore such American derivatives as Monterey, Santa Barbara and Nantucket. And, looking further, we began to express a clearer and cleaner version of the Craftsman, the Shingle, the Ranch and the American Farmhouse. All of this was done that we might better execute what has become known as "The New California Tradition"—a rich yet diverse new vocabulary.

But our task is far from over. Like no other place, California challenges us with constant change. Socio-economic and demographic forces continually alter the entire process of household formation, resulting in new definitions of interior spaces and better relationships between private and public zones. As the Golden State's demand for higher single-family detached density and more innovative attached-home solutions escalates, the price of its land grows ever dearer. New building techniques and eco-friendly materials such as steel, plastic and foam are being introduced, along with a call for better use of sustainable and renewable elements.

Change is the driving force. Change is part of the reason couturiers, actors, culinary artists, musicians and even auto designers from across the globe sink roots here; they want to be close to the stunningly powerful dynamism of California's mix. For them as for us, this land boasts an endless capacity for evolution and fusion.

Fusion. California—our backyard and our marketplace—calls daily for it. Revise tradition, reinvent it; create a better breed, a new mix. Remake architecture to reflect and respond to Left Coast ethnic and economic shifts—make it rhyme.

We now see that "the home of the future is the house of the past" is itself about to pass. The last decade's evolution of residential design has brought Bassenian/Lagoni Architects, as well as the homebuyer, through a much-deepened understanding of the past—a keener sense of what counts, a maturation of taste. Austrian-born L.A. chef Wolfgang Puck adeptly fuses French and Japanese cooking traditions with fresh California ingredients—denying cultural boundaries while simultaneously glorying in the culinary history of each locale. In like manner, today's California architect must evolve a new residential design—educe a new recipe—via the sure-handed fusion of distinct traditions, expressing function and form in a more substantial contemporary style.

The good design for the not-so-distant future will be complex in origin and concepts, yet cleaner, more sculptural and simple of line. More focused. More flexible. It will derive from a *dis*-covering, a *de*-layering of much of the stylistic cosmetics accumulated over the centuries. As a sculptor finds the form within the stone, we seek to release the full-bore energy of architecture's form—to free it of unyielding authenticism. By so doing, we hope to attain the multi-traditional vantage point necessary for the powerful fusion that becomes the new home.

Annotated Projects List
Completed Work

Arden Square
Residences One & Two
Irvine, California
2001 – 2002
Pages 134-135

Bassenian/Lagoni Architects Team:
Land Planner: Scott Adams, AICP
Designer: Craig Gambill, AIA
Project Manager: Jeff Roach

Builder: Brookfield Homes
Builder Executive in Charge of Design:
   Adrian Foley
Landscape Architect: Summers/Murphy
   & Partners
Interior Designer: Design Tec Interiors
Structural Engineer: Dale Christian

Photographer: Jeffrey Aron (2001)

Awards:
Gold Nuggets 2002
   Grand Award (Residence Four)
   Merit Awards (Residences One & Two)
MAME/Southern California 2001
   Finalist (Residence Two)

Balboa Peninsula Residence
Newport Beach, California
2001
Pages 100-103

Bassenian/Lagoni Architects Team:
Designer: Steven Dewan, AIA
Project Manager: Mike Beam

Builder: Warmington Homes
Structural Engineer: Dale Christian

Photographer: John Bare (2001)

Awards:
Best in American Living Awards 2001
   Gold Award
Gold Nuggets 2001
   Merit Award

Classics at Hopkins Place
Palo Alto, California
1996 – 1997
Pages 138-139

Bassenian/Lagoni Architects Team:
Designer: Steven Dewan, AIA
Project Manager: Ken Niemerski, AIA

Builder: Classic Communities
Builder Executive in Charge of Design:
   Scott Ward
Structural Engineer: Gouvis Engineering

Photographer: John Bare (1996)

Awards:
Best in American Living Awards 1996
   Grand Award—Best Community
Gold Nuggets 1997
   Merit Award—Best Infill Community

Clifton Heights
Residence Two
Ladera Ranch, California
2002
Pages 116-119

Bassenian/Lagoni Architects Team:
Designer: Dave Kosco, AIA
Project Manager: Jeff Marcotte

Builder: Centex Homes—South Coast
   Division
Builder Executive in Charge of Design:
   Nick Lehnert
Landscape Architect: Land Concern, Ltd.
Interior Designer: Rooms Interiors
Structural Engineer: Gouvis Engineering

Photographer: Eric Figge (2002)

Awards:
Gold Nuggets 2002
   Merit Award

The Colony at Bridgeport
Valencia, California
2001 – 2002
Pages 136-137

Bassenian/Lagoni Architects Team:
Land Planner: Scott Adams, AICP
Designer: Kevin Karami
Project Manager: Roberta Jeannette

Builder: Centex Homes – LA/Ventura
Division
Builder Executive in Charge of Design:
Mark Higgins
Landscape Architect: LANTEX Landscape
Architecture
Interior Designer: Creative Design
Consultants
Structural Engineer: Performance Plus

Photographer: Robb Miller (2001)

Awards:
Best in American Living Awards 2001
Silver Awards (Residences One &
Three)
National Sales & Marketing Awards 2001
Silver Finalist—Detached Community
of the Year
Silver Finalist & Regional Winner
(Residence Three)
Gold Nuggets 2001
Merit Award—Residential Detached
Project 9 Units/Acre or More
Merit Awards (Residences One &
Three)
Elan Awards 2001
Winner—Community of the Year
Winners (Residences One & Three)
Finalist (Residence Two)
MAME/Southern California 2001
Finalist (Residence Three)

Heritage Walk
Pasadena, California
1999 – 2000
Pages 60-61

Bassenian/Lagoni Architects Team:
Designers: Dave Kosco, AIA, and
Kevin Karami
Project Manager: Brian Neves, AIA

Builder: The Olson Company
Builder Executive in Charge of Design:
Mark Buckland
Landscape Architect: The Collaborative
West
Interior Designer: Design Tec Interiors
Structural Engineer: Gouvis Engineering

Photographer: Eric Figge (2000)

Awards:
Best in American Living Awards 2000
Winner—Best Attached 9 Units/Acre
or More (Residence Three)
Finalist—Best Affordable Plan
(Residence One)
Builders Choice 2000
Finalist (Residence One)
National Sales & Marketing 2000
Finalist—Attached Community of
the Year
Finalist (Residence Three)
Gold Nuggets 2000
Grand Award—Attached Community of
the Year
Grand Award—Best Infill Site Plan
Grand Award (Residence One)
Merit Awards (Residences Two &
Three)
MAME/Southern California 2000
Finalist—Attached Community of
the Year
Finalist (Residences One & Three)

Laguna Beach Residence
Emerald Bay, California
1995
Pages 90-99

Bassenian/Lagoni Architects Team:
Designers: Aram Bassenian, AIA;
Jim Lind, AIA; Kevin Karami
Project Manager: Yoon Lee & Associates

Builder: Akins Construction
Landscape Architect: Grisamore Design
Interior Designer: Saddleback
Interiors/Jeff Benedick
Structural Engineer: Gouvis Engineering

Photographer: John Bare (1997)

Awards:
Gold Nuggets 1997
Merit Award

Lighthouse at The Boardwalk
Residences One & Two
Huntington Beach, California
2001 – 2002
Pages 126-133

Bassenian/Lagoni Architects Team:
Designer: Dave Kosco, AIA
Project Manager: Jeff Marcotte

Builder: Christopher Homes
Builder Executive in Charge of Design:
Chris Gibbs
Landscape Architect: Summers/Murphy
& Partners
Interior Designer: Saddleback Interiors
Structural Engineer: Gouvis Engineering

Photographer: John Bare (2002)

Awards:
Gold Nuggets 2002
Merit Awards (Residences One & Two)

Montellano
Residence Three
San Clemente, California
2002
Pages 46-49

Bassenian/Lagoni Architects Team:
Designer: Dave Pockett
Project Manager: Lenz Casilan

Builder: William Lyon Homes
Builder Executive in Charge of Design:
 Tom Grable
Landscape Architect: Frank Radmacher
 Associates
Interior Designer: Creative Design
 Consultants
Structural Engineer: Infinity Design Group

Photographer: Eric Figge (2002)

Sandover
Residence One
Huntington Beach, California
2000 – 2001
Pages 104-105

Bassenian/Lagoni Architects Team:
Designer: Ray Hart
Project Manager: Mike Beam

Builder: Hearthside Homes
Builder Executive in Charge of Design:
 Mike Rafferty
Landscape Architect: Land Concern, Ltd.
Interior Designer: Design Tec Interiors
Structural Engineer: Infinity Design Group

Photographer: Jeffrey Aron (2001)

Santa Barbara
Residence Three
San Diego, California
2002
Pages 50-55

Bassenian/Lagoni Architects Team:
Designer: Ernie Gorrill, AIA
Project Manager: Scott Bunney

Builder: Pardee Homes
Builder Executive in Charge of Design:
 Bob Clauser
Landscape Architect: Land Concern, Ltd.
Interior Designer: Color Design Art
Structural Engineer: Borm Associates

Photographer: Jeff Smith (2002)

Awards:
 Gold Nuggets 2002
 Finalist

Serena
Residences Two & Three
Newport Coast, California
1999 – 2000
Pages 40-43, 80-83

Bassenian/Lagoni Architects Team:
Designer: Kevin Karami
Project Manager: Brian Neves, AIA

Builder: Shea Homes
Builder Executive in Charge of Design:
 Les Thomas
Landscape Architect: Lifescapes
 International
Interior Designer: Pacific Dimensions
Structural Engineer: ESI/FME Engineering

Photographer: Jeffrey Aron (1999)

Awards:
 Best in American Living Awards 2000
 Gold Award (Residence Three)
 Gold Nuggets 2000
 Merit Award (Residence Three)
 MAME/Southern California 1999
 Finalist (Residence Three)

Shoreline at The Boardwalk
Residences One & Two
Huntington Beach, California
2001 – 2002
Pages 106-115

Bassenian/Lagoni Architects Team:
Designer: Dave Kosco, AIA
Project Manager: Jeff Marcotte

Builder: Christopher Homes
Builder Executive in Charge of Design:
  Chris Gibbs
Landscape Architect: Summers /
  Murphy & Partners
Interior Designer: Saddleback Interiors
Structural Engineer: Gouvis
  Engineering

Photographer: John Bare (2002)

Awards:
  Gold Nuggets 2002
    Merit Award (Residence One)

Silver Creek
Residence Two
Coto de Caza, California
2000 – 2001
Pages 56-59

Bassenian/Lagoni Architects Team:
Designer: Kevin Karami
Project Manager: Gerry Esser

Builder: Lennar Homes
Builder Executive in Charge of Design:
  Tom Martin
Landscape Architect: Summers /
Murphy & Partners
Interior Designer: Chameleon
  Merchandising & Design
Structural Engineer: Dale Christian

Photographer: John Bare (2000)

Awards:
  Gold Nuggets 2000
    Merit Award

Somerton
Residence Four
Irvine, California
1999 – 2000
Pages 44-45

Bassenian/Lagoni Architects Team:
Designer: Hans Anderle
Project Manager: Mike Beam

Builder: Standard Pacific Homes
Builder Executives in Charge of Design:
  Scott Stowell and Gary Carlson
Landscape Architect: HRP LanDesign
Interior Designer: Saddleback Interiors
Structural Engineer: Infinity Design
  Group

Photographer: John Bare (1999)

Awards:
  Best in American Living Awards
    1999 Finalist

Southern Hills
Residence Two
Coto de Caza, California
1998 – 1999
Pages 120-123

Bassenian/Lagoni Architects Team:
Designer: Kevin Karami
Project Manager: Gerry Esser

Builder: Lennar Homes
Builder Executives in Charge of Design:
  Jeff Roos and Tom Martin
Landscape Architect: Summers /
  Murphy & Partners
Interior Designer: Karen Butera
Structural Engineer: Dale Christian

Photographer: John Bare (1998)

Awards:
  Gold Nuggets 1998
    Merit Award
  MAME/Orange County 1998
    Finalist

Tesoro Crest
Residence Two
Newport Coast, California
1998 – 1999
Pages 84-85

Bassenian/Lagoni Architects Team:
Designers: Dave Kosco, AIA, and Steven
  Dewan, AIA
Project Manager: Sophia Braverman

Builder: Standard Pacific Homes
Builder Executives in Charge of Design:
  Scott Stowell and Gary Carlson
Landscape Architect: HRP LanDesign
Interior Designer: Saddleback Interiors
Structural Engineer: Dale Christian

Photographer: John Bare (1998)

Awards:
  Best in American Living Awards 1998
    Platinum
  Gold Nuggets 1998
    Merit Award

Triana
Residence Two
Escondido, California
1999 – 2000
Pages 86-87

Bassenian/Lagoni Architects Team:
Designer: Dave Kosco, AIA
Project Manager: Mike Beam

Builder: Hearthside Homes
Builder Executive in Charge of Design:
  Mike Rafferty
Landscape Architect: Land Concern, Ltd.
Interior Designer: Design Tec Interiors
Structural Engineer: Infinity Design Group

Photographer: Jeffrey Aron (2000)

Awards:
  Gold Nuggets 2000
    Grand Award
  MAME/Southern California
    Finalist

Villas at The Bridges
Residences One, Two & Three
Rancho Santa Fe, California
2001 – 2002
Pages 64-79

Bassenian/Lagoni Architects Team:
Designer: Dave Kosco, AIA
Project Manager: Marty Lopez

Builder: Lennar Homes
Builder Executive in Charge of Design:
  Tom Martin
Landscape Architect: Pinnacle Design
  Co.
Interior Designer: Pacific Dimensions
Structural Engineer: Borm Associates

Photographer: Eric Figge (2002)
  Doug Smith (2002) (Page 79 only)

Awards:
  Gold Nuggets 2002
    Grand Award (Residence One)
    Merit Awards (Residences Two &
      Three)

Windward at Crystal Cove
Residences One, Two, Three & Four
Newport Beach, California
2000 – 2001
Pages 14-39

Bassenian/Lagoni Architects Team:
Designer: Kevin Karami
Project Manager: Brian Neves, AIA

Builder: Richmond American
Builder Executive in Charge of Design:
  Robert Shiota
Landscape Architect: The Collaborative
  West
Interior Designer: Pacific Dimensions
Structural Engineer: Option One
  Engineering

Photographer: Eric Figge (2001)

Awards:
  Best in American Living Awards 2001
    Platinum Award (Residences Two,
      Three & Four)
    Silver Award—Detached Community
      of the Year
  Gold Nuggets 2001
    Grand Award (Residence One)
    Merit Awards (Residences Two,
      Three & Four)
  MAME/Southern California 2000
    Finalist—Detached Community of
      Year
    Finalist (Residences Two, Three &
      Four)

Annotated Projects List
On-The-Board

Shady Canyon Custom Residence
Irvine, California
2002
Page 142

Bassenian/Lagoni Architects:
Designer: Kevin Karami
Project Manager: Gerry Esser

Builder: Warmington Homes
Builder Executive in Charge of Design:
 Matt White

Benchley Hill at Amerige Heights
Residence Two
Fullerton, California
2002
Page 143

Bassenian/Lagoni Architects:
Designer: John Bigot
Project Manager: Roberta Jeannette

Builder: Pardee Homes
Builder Executive in Charge of Design:
 Bob Clauser

The Ranch at Santa Monica
Residences Two & Four
San Diego, California
Pages 144, 145

Bassenian/Lagoni Architects:
Designers: Craig Gambill
Project Manager: Jeff Marcotte

Builder: Western Pacific Housing
Builder Executive in Charge of Design:
 Lance Waite

Renaissance
Residences One & Two
Novato, CA
2002
Pages 146, 147

Bassenian/Lagoni Architects:
Designer: Kevin Karami
Project Manager: Sophia Braverman

Builder: Davidon Homes
Builder Executive in Charge of Design:
 Don Chaiken

Digital Imagery: Focus 360 Architectural
 Communications

Shady Canyon
Residences One & Two
Irvine, California
2002
Pages 148,149

Bassenian/Lagoni Architects:
Designer: Dave Kosco, AIA, and
 Kevin Karami
Project Manager: Jeff Marcotte

Builder: Greystone Homes
Builder Executive in Charge of Design:
 Tom Martin

Staff 2002

Executive Staff
Aram Bassenian
Carl Lagoni
Scott Adams
Dave Kosco
Jeff LaFetra
Lee Rogaliner

Vice Presidents
Mike Beam
Steven Dewan
Kevin Karami
Jeff Lake
Ken Niemerski

Associate Vice Presidents
Ernie Gorrill
Brian Neves
Dave Pockett

Associates
Hans Anderle
Sophia Braverman
David Day
Gerry Esser
Judy Forrester
Craig Gambill
Jeff Ganyo
Ray Hart
Marty Lopez
Jeff Marcotte
Edie Motoyama
Wendy Woolsey

General Staff
Joe Abrajano
Jose Alvarez
Stacie Arrigo
John Bigot
Randy Brown
Scott Bunney
Kevin Burt
Dwayne Butz
Brian Cameron
Lenz Casilan
Luis Chavez
Dana Cline
Jennifer Cram
Susan Dewan
Kele Dooley
Dee Drylie
Maleck Elahi
Elmer Evangelista
Kim Evdakiou
Clois Fitch
Matthew Finn
Diane Galin
Mike Gilbert
Javier Gomez
Simon Ha
George Handy
Elian Hernandez
Jenaro Hernandez
Young Hong
Bryce Hove
Roberta Jeannette
Sopida Ketmanee-Flores
Christa Lewis
Angie Manriques
Kristina McVeigh

Tom Mkhitaryan
Andy Moehring
Justin Myers
Christopher Ngo
Khoa Nguyen
Jo Ann O'Neill
Curtis Ong
John Oravetz
Debby Owens
Margo Penick
Mike Pilarski
Heather Pilling
Bob Platt
Yvonne Ramos
Ben Regalado
Nate Rodholm
Ryan Rosecrans
Jeffry Sinarjo
Marshall Smith
Ian Sparks
Melissa Spence
Tony Taylor
Courtney Tran
Linda Vancil
Chris Velasquez
Tony Vinh
Warren Walker
David Wang
Ryan White
Stacy White
Eric Widmer
John Wilmert
Jason Yaw
Albern Yolo
Bernard Yuen

Index